The Buddhist Way of Life

The Buddhist
Way of Life

CHRISTMAS HUMPHREYS

London
Published for the Buddhist Society by
GEORGE ALLEN AND UNWIN LTD
RUSKIN HOUSE MUSEUM STREET

FIRST PUBLISHED IN 1969

SBN 04 294059 1

PRINTED IN GREAT BRITAIN
in 11 on 12 point Juliana type
BY THE BLACKFRIARS PRESS LTD
LEICESTER

Dedicated to the Past, Present and
Future Members of the Buddhist
Society, London

Preface

This book was planned some years ago on the lines of my *Studies in the Middle Way* which had been in print already for some twenty years. The contents were drafted, a number of chapters written, and considerable notes prepared for many more. Then for some reason the folder was laid aside and its material became, as is the fate of many unfinished works, a quarry for later articles and lectures.

In the result, when I returned to the subject I had to collect a number of articles from journals in all parts of the world, and to extract from the tape-recordings of lectures the substance of what I had left as notes for chapters. A few independent articles and talks have also been included as further contributions to the same theme of Buddhism applied to daily life. For Buddhism, though usually referred to as a religion, and replete with a magnificent range of philosophy, metaphysics, mysticism, psychology, ritual, morality and culture, is basically, it seems to me, a way of life. Upon this Way all aspects of the human mind have relevance, but the dedicated Buddhist is ever concerned with the Way itself which leads, so he finds from experience, to Enlightenment for himself and all mankind.

In this belief I have concentrated my own study and writing on the actual practice of Buddhist principles, making use the criterion of value. To this end I wrote *Walk On!*, *The Buddhist Way of Action*, *Zen, a Way of Life* and other works, and have made the same emphasis in countless articles and talks.

But the application of a set of principles to daily life is not a matter of straightforward thinking, as the exposition of the principles may be. The conditioning of the individual, his education, mental make-up and cultural environment, the balance of his mind's development in terms of intellect and feeling and intuitive development, all these are relevant, and his approach to what Marcus Aurelius called 'the ambit of one's moral purpose' will be at all times multiple. It will include digression and even retraction, and the same point may be studied from many points of view before intellectual acceptance is matured into spiritual growth.

No apology, therefore, is made for overlapping and repetition in the chapters which follow. When a Western mind attempts to understand, deeply and thoroughly, the basic principles of an Eastern way of life, there is much to do, and a wide field of literature, scriptures, text-books and articles, representing a hundred points of view, must be absorbed and digested. From such a synthesis of doctrine and methods the enquirer's mind moves nearer to spiritual experience and the proffered way of life. The West may prefer a straight and logical path from accumulated facts to reasonable inference therefrom; the East moves differently, and I have a mind which prefers the Eastern point of view.

In nearly fifty years' study of Buddhism I have used all means of approach to understanding. To intellect I have added a blend of feeling, intuition and applied psychology, and happily use tradition, analogy, and also consistency with that 'accumulated Wisdom of the ages' which I believe to be the common heritage of the great Teachers of mankind. And using, as my ego lets me, the wise addition of patience and humility, I read again and again, from a dozen points of view, the doctrines which I wish to understand, until the hard walls of preconception begin to waver and fall before the repeated battering of a new idea.

I repeat, therefore, that I do not apologize for saying the same thing many times, for thus have I learnt what little I know. May the following chapters help the reader to tread that Middle Way proclaimed by Gautama the Buddha which leads, as I have found, as far as one has strength to tread towards that Light of wisdom-love which is ever here and now, and waits but our unveiling.

I have added a few poems. I firmly believe that at times I say more in a sonnet than in an essay, and 'Beyond' is in a sense, though highly compressed and at times elliptical in expression, the distillation of a lifetime's study.

I am grateful to the editors of the following journals in which some of this material has appeared: the *American Theosophist*, the *Aryan Path*, the *Buddhist Annual* of Ceylon, the Journal of the Maha Bodhi Society and the *Middle Way*, the journal of the Buddhist Society, London.

I am equally grateful to all those ladies who have retyped material for me. If at times, in attempting to read my written improvements, they have produced remarks and doctrines utterly new to me, the fault was ever mine, and I have at times adopted their exciting rendering.

T.C.H.

St John's Wood
New Year, 1968

Contents

DEEPER TRUTHS OF BUDDHISM

ZEN BUDDHISM

Background

I

The Purpose of Buddhism

Buddhism is a system of doctrine and practice built up by the followers of the Buddha about what they believed to be his teaching, but the purpose of Buddhism is a state of consciousness known as Enlightenment. We do not know precisely what the Buddha taught, for nothing was written down, but his words were committed to memory by those trained to remember, and two things at least are for the practising Buddhist beyond argument. He himself attained supreme Enlightenment, and he taught the Way to it to all mankind.

For Gautama Siddhartha became the Buddha when he became, and was acknowledged to have become, *buddha*, 'enlightened' or 'awakened'; more, he was the *fully* Awakened One, who had shattered the power of self, broken the fetters of the thinking mind, and made his consciousness one with universal consciousness. While in that state his wisdom was absolute, and his range of compassion commensurate with all that lives. He was therefore at the same time the All-Compassionate One. These twin facets of his cosmic consciousness must both be realized. As Dr Suzuki has said, 'There are two pillars supporting the great edifice of Buddhism; Mahaprajna, great Wisdom, and Mahakaruna, great Compassion. The wisdom flows from the compassion and the compassion from the wisdom, for the two are one.'[1]

But Gautama Siddhartha was a man, not a god, still less God, and what one man has done other men may do. But how? By

[1] *The Essence of Buddhism*, D. T. Suzuki, p. 40.

treading in the footsteps of this extra-ordinary man, the long and difficult path which he described from suffering to the end of suffering, from limited mind to No-mind, from the world of the born and formed to the 'Unborn, Unformed', from relative to absolute awareness.

This, then, is the heart of Buddhism, and all, in the last analysis, that we need. The rest, of doctrine and belief, of meditation exercises, ritual and rules of life, is either of help on the way to Enlightenment, or a waste of time. It lies in the field of duality, while Enlightenment lies 'beyond', in the state of awareness known as Non-duality, for it is beyond both Many and One. We study doctrine, but why? We meditate, but why? The only good reason is to prepare the mind for a break-through to No-mind. To study doctrine without applying it in daily life may satisfy the scholar but is contrary to the very words of Buddhist scripture. To collect a range of untested belief is to collect a row of Buddhist images with which to adorn the mantelshelf; the Buddhist is otherwise engaged. He is urgent to find the end of suffering, and once he has entered the Way he has but a single thought—in the words of a Zen master, to 'walk on!' His way is the direct way; his experience is sought first-hand. When a man by mistake puts his hand into boiling water he pulls it out and yells with pain. This is direct experience. When for the first time he falls in love, that is direct experience. So is the first 'moment', a moment out of time, of 'enlightenment', as direct, unmistakable, unforgettable but indescribable as any other direct experience.

How do we contact Reality? Not with the intellect. The thinking, rational, daily mind for ever functions in duality, in the relative. By it we learn a great deal about the universe and the 'matter'—which has now been found to have, as the Buddha said, no real existence—of which it is composed. But this knowledge is entirely 'about it and about'; it concerns the forms in which life is expressed, the garments of Reality; the life, the essence, the thing itself it can never know. The scientist, the philosopher, the psychologist, and all who work with the five senses and thought may fill the world with libraries of their invention and discovery; they will not, for they cannot, *know*.

We know what we do know of Reality with a different

faculty, as different and distinct from thought or feeling as either is from the scent of a rose. In the East it is known as *buddhi*, from the same root as *buddha*; in the West as the intuition, the 'immediate apprehension by the mind without reasoning', as the dictionary says. It is the faculty in man by which he attunes his limited human consciousness to the spark of the Light, or Spirit, or the Buddha within. There is, as we know from Buddhist teaching, no unchanging or immortal soul in man which is in the true sense *his*. But this light of the Unborn is in every man for each and all to use; the intuition is, as it were, a built-in receiving set by which and by which alone his 'mind' in the total sense may learn to know its individual unity—or nonduality—with the nameless No-thingness which lies 'beyond'.

If this be right, the Buddhist must not only tread the Middle Way in terms of doctrine, motive, morality and mind-development, but look ahead to the first appearance of that enlightenment which is the purpose of this long subjective journey. This seems to involve developing the dormant faculty of the intuition. But how? The intellect can be exercised at will and so developed with deliberate use through many lives that it becomes the magnificent instrument which is at present man's supreme achievement. But how can we develop the intuition, how woo these fugitive and unexpected glimpses of Reality to come again? Clearly we cannot yet command them, but we can, I believe, increase the power of this light within. Remembering that the aspects of the mind are in no sense separate, but facets of an instrument of vast complexity, we can deliberately work to illumine the processes of thought which cannot by themselves achieve Reality with the light of *buddhi* which can, for it functions on the plane of that we seek, the Unborn Reality. But this soft process of irradiation first suffuses the higher ranges of mind, the power of abstract synthesis and large relationship. It seems that the 'higher' we reach in thought the more our thought is illumined, frequently if not at will, by the light of what Buddhists call Enlightenment, or spiritual awakening, or cosmic consciousness. This power of synthesis implies expansion, a progressive enlargement of scope, and this in turn involves the simultaneous apprehension of conflicting thoughts. Lighted up with the light of the Unborn which, shining everywhere, is picked up by the receiving set of the intuition, it can even include antithetical points of view, sheer opposites, so that we understand by what has been called Zen logic that A is A and also at the same time not-A, and indeed, in the final triumph of super-rational attainment, that A is A *because* A is not-A, which explains, as Dr Suzuki says, why God created the universe.

This is a difficult climb, but we shall not begin to grasp the meaning of Enlightenment until we follow the All-Awakened One beyond the region of thought, beyond the false duality of self and not-self, true and untrue, good and evil. However good we may become, or clever, we remain in the foothills of our climbing. The Light is only seen when the fog of duality thins enough to allow for occasional flashes, but the quality of these sudden glimpses is unmistakable. In these brief 'moments' there is no knower who knows, no self to feel pride in achievement, no knowledge gained; only a powerful sense of certainty, of immense serenity, of oneness with and compassion for all other forms of life, the one life of the Unborn, that harmony which is the universe.

If we cannot command these glimpses of the Light we can provide the conditions in which it is more likely that they will appear. By reading and brooding over the spiritually exciting words of the great masters we stimulate the mind to waken to their truth; by opening the heart to the cry of all who suffer we remove the sense of a separate self which stands so drearily, so wearily and to the end so subtly in our way. By learning to 'walk on' with no other end in view than more and more expansion, growth and hence enlightenment we enter the Path, merge with the Path, become the Path which leads to it. Thus we are Buddhists, striving for that state of consciousness we call Enlightenment, and we know no greater glory than to be worthy of that name.

2

The Field of Buddhism

Buddhism today represents the largest field of thought in the known history of mankind. Its components are partly visible and partly invisible, the former including a long and complex story of 2,500 years of development combined with what may be called the geography of Buddhism; in the course of time at least a dozen countries, races and cultures came under its sway, and its story and scriptures are written in at least seven different languages.

The invisible factors include its doctrines, its many schools and its methods of meditation; this field is still developing in width and depth, and though links may be found with Western science, psychology and sociology, in many cases Buddhist scriptures show that these modern 'discoveries' have been taught for at least two thousand years.

At the heart of Buddhism lies the conviction that Gautama Siddhartha became Buddha, the Enlightened One, and the search for this enlightenment is the goal of all Buddhists. The life of the prince who gave up everything to seek the cause of suffering and the way to remove it is well known to every Buddhist; here we are more concerned with the field of thought which developed from his simple teaching of the Way—the Way which leads to the heart's peace when once all thought of self is dead. He taught this Way for fifty years, and when he died his message was already known throughout the length and breadth of north-east India.

The message spread; to Ceylon by the hand of Asoka's children, Mahinda and Sanghamitta, who in 252 B.C. planted a slip of the Bo-tree which may be seen today. To Burma and

Thailand, and down the archipelago to Cambodia and Java. Then East, along the trade routes to China, Korea and Japan, and West to the Hellenic-influenced tribes of Afghanistan. Then North to Tibet and thence Mongolia. But by A.D. 1000 the movement had ceased: in India the great University of Nalanda still flourished, but soon with the rest of Buddhism it went down before the swordpoint of Islam.

But that which survived and developed in the lands about India was not any more one Buddhism. No teaching which expressly allows its followers to explore all aspects of the mind is likely to remain of one school only, and in the long years of its history Buddhism has happily flowed into a dozen or more channels of thought and practice. Yet all retain three factors in common: the Buddha, as the All-Enlightened One; a large body of doctrine and practice; and a quite remarkable tolerance of differing points of view. There has never been a Buddhist war, nor has any man been killed or even injured by a Buddhist for holding a different point of view. Let us then, look briefly at these schools of Buddhism, at their scriptures and at the men who wrote them.

The earliest school on record is the Hinayana, which by the third century B.C. had split into eighteen sects. Of these only one has survived, the Theravada or doctrine of the Elders, found today in Ceylon, Burma, Siam and Cambodia. Its Canon is complete, much having been written down in the first century B.C.— all of it is available in English, thanks to the work of the Pali Text Society. Lying as it does on the fringe of the Buddhist world, this school was unaffected by development elsewhere, and is still, in doctrine and practice, built about the Sangha. But early in the history of Buddhism there was dissension at the great Councils called from time to time to settle and preserve the Doctrine, and already by the second century B.C. we find in two other schools of the Hinayana the seeds of the later views and practices which together formed the magnificent palace of thought which is known as the Mahayana.

Great scriptures continued to be written in India for centuries after the Theravada had found its home in Ceylon. A group of great importance was the Prajna-paramita literature, concerning 'the Wisdom which has gone beyond'; two famous summaries are the Diamond and the Heart Sutras. All are concerned with Sunyata, the doctrine of the Plenum-Void, which is the Theravada doctrine of Anatta carried to its ultimate limits. About the same time appeared the Maha-Parinirvana Sutra, with the developed teaching of the Bodhisattva, the famous Lotus of the Good Law Sutra (Saddharmapundarika), about which two entire schools, the Tendai and Nichiren, were later founded, and the two Sukhavati Sutras which developed the teaching of the Pure Land, later to become the largest school in Japan. All these themes and ideas developed from seeds already visible in sects of the Hinayana School, and all were eagerly debated in the great University of Nalanda, where for nearly a thousand years the greatest minds of the East taught and debated the doctrines of Buddhism.

From this mass of learning there slowly crystallized two major schools of Mahayana Buddhism. One of the greatest minds of India, Nagarjuna, in the second century A.D. founded (or at least systematized) the Madhyamika School as a 'Middle Way' between the prevailing views of Existence and Non-existence concerning visible and invisible phenomena. To solve the problem an Absolute and a Relative Truth were admitted, but behind both lies the Sunyata of the Prajna-paramita literature. Later, in the fifth century, these metaphysical doctrines were transferred to the field of psychology by the brothers Vasubandhu and Asanga, who between them crystallized the views of the Yogacara or Vijnanavada School of Mind-Only. In their foremost Scripture, the Lankavatara Sutra, the Buddha becomes a cosmic principle of Buddhahood; the doctrine of his three Bodies (Trikaya) is displayed, and in the Alaya-Vijnana, the 'Store-consciousness', appears the psychological forerunner of the Unconscious of Western psychology. Another great Scripture is the vast Avatamsaka Sutra, but better known is the Awakening of Faith, thanks to the early translation by Dr Suzuki (1900).

These doctrines and schools took a long time to develop, but for a thousand years (300 B.C. to A.D. 700) they had the benefit of Buddhist rulers such as the Emperor Asoka, King Kanishka of the Kushans in the North-West, and King Harsha in the North-East, in whose shadow they could grow. Buddhist art was able to thrive; the semi-Hellenic art of Gandhara in the North-

West, the lovely art of the Mathura School under the Gupta Dynasty, and the spiritual faces of the images of North-East India which were produced under the Pala kings. Groups of cave-dwellings were slowly carved out through the centuries from mere Stupas, or relic-mounds, to lecture halls with rock-cut Viharas for the monks. In Bhilsa, Barhut and Sanchi and later at Ajanta, Ellora and Karli, we can trace in existing ruins the lives and longings of the bhikkhus and laymen of that day.

Still the great names appeared and great Scriptures were written—by Santideva in the seventh century, in the dialogues we know as the Questions of King Milinda, and in the Surangama Sutra which, however, is perhaps Chinese. Meanwhile, the Abhidhamma of the surviving Theravada School was developed in Ceylon, and the Sutta Nipata and Dhammapada, early works now famous the world over, were written down and made the subject of commentaries. But the sun of Indian Buddhism was setting. Whatever the causes of its decline in India, the swords of Islam destroyed the monasteries and those who lived in them, and when the Sangha went the Teaching followed.

But Indian thought was not a closed circuit. The trade routes to the East carried more than merchandise; they carried ideas as well. Early in the 2nd century Buddhism arrived in China, perhaps with the Sutra of 42 Sections, a Hinayana work. By the time of Kumarajiva (fifth century) the task of translating the Indian Sutras was in full swing, and schools were founded about them. A curious blend of the old and the new took place, and out of the mixture came purely Chinese schools. The Tientai (Jap. Tendai) was centred about the Lotus Sutra, while about the Avatamsaka Sutra was gathered a group of minds which, in the Kegon-Shu of Japan, produced some of the greatest philosophy of the world. The Pure Land teaching of the Sukhavati Sutras formed the heart of the Jodo School (which in Japan was carried to its limits in the Shin-Shu), while the uncompromising directness of Bodhidharma founded, with the aid of his great followers of the Ch'an tradition, the Sudden School of direct enlightenment known today in Japan as Zen.

Meanwhile a series of Chinese pilgrims, Fa-hien, Hiuen-Tsang and I-Tsing, brought back an increasing quantity of Indian texts, all of which were translated, studied and in turn applied to methods of self-enlightenment. Between them they encouraged and produced some of the world's greatest art—that of the T'ang Dynasty (seventh to tenth century), which in the view of many has never been surpassed.

The message spread to Japan. First in the seventh century, when Buddhism was adopted by Prince Shotoku at his capital of Nara, and then in Kyoto where, from the eighth century on-wards, were produced some of the greatest schools, scriptures and minds in the whole field of Buddhism. All the Chinese schools were brought over and new ones were founded. Ch'an became Zen, in its two forms, Rinzai and Soto; Jodo was developed into Shin; Tendai and Kegon developed from their Chinese counterparts, and Nichiren founded the movement of his name, to adore the Lotus Sutra as Wisdom incarnate in words.

The Tantric beliefs and practices of India passed through the Mantra School of Peking to become the Shingon of Japan, and in the Ritsu School even the Vinaya discipline was practised for centuries. Japanese art and culture developed accordingly, the Samurai preferring Zen, the people preferring Shin and the scholars developing the schools of thought of Tendai and Kegon. From these and the Japanese love of beauty came the Tea Ceremony and Flower Arrangement; Judo and Kendo and Bushido adopted the cult of Zen. Today the Shin sect has the greatest numbers, but Zen holds the spiritual strength which reflects the virility of the nation, and which has power to affect the Western mind.

Meanwhile the message was carried North, into Tibet in the eighth century by Padmasambhava and those who followed him, and thence into Mongolia. Three strains of Buddhism were taken in; the Vinaya discipline, the principles of the Yogacara School and the Tantras of Bengal. All were blended in the Tibetan mind, which also had the Prajnaparamita scriptures to study and apply. Schools were founded, reformed and allowed to die, as in the other countries where Buddhism had spread. Then the Gelug-pa, or Reformed movement of Tsongkha-pa became dominant, and includes today the Dalai and the Panchen Lamas. The pantheon grew under Tantric influence; heights of spirituality in pure experience were attained by some, even as the lowest ranks of the people were sunk in sorcery and psychic practices but little removed from the indigenous religion of Bön. Here again the art of the country is Buddhist, the thankas and images alike conforming to a rigid ecclesiastical discipline.

So, by the fifteenth century the picture is reasonably complete. In Ceylon, Siam, Burma and Cambodia, the Theravada with its Sangha of yellow-robed bhikkhus and its complete Canon in Pali. In Tibet, a Tibetan Buddhism, a blend of many schools, and an Order which, having much in common with the older Sangha, is yet more of a Church. In Japan, the Order as such never claimed the authority which obtains in the Sangha proper. There are monks but also priests who marry and return to the world. In doctrine there is vast variety, including all those factors set out earlier herein. None alone is Buddhism; none claims to be. Much is at the heart of Buddhism, the group of doctrines common to all schools. But at the edge of the circle, as it widened through the centuries, are beliefs and practices which seem remote from the centre. What would the Buddha have said to Tantric ritual, or to the pure faith of Shin? But that, says the Buddhist, is not the question, for the attitude to the Buddha himself has changed. Nowhere have the 'accidents' of history less importance than in Buddhism. Buddhism would not today be troubled if some great mind should prove that the Buddha as a man never lived at all. Buddhism is a way, and so long as there are men who seek a Way from sorrow to Enlightenment, it will exist for those who tread it.

Buddhism came West, back to India whence it had been expelled in the tenth to twelfth centuries. In the work of the Maha Bodhi Society, which has centres in all the great cities, and in the work of the late Dr Ambedkar among the 'untouchables', there are signs of a movement which may yet profoundly affect the face of India. But Buddhism continued West, to Europe and the USA. A great range of Buddhist Scripture is now available in English; text-books on every corner of the field are appearing every year. There are societies large and small all over Europe; in England the movement began in 1907 and has since grown steadily. The same applies to the USA which, though behind in literature, is now catching up. As a factor in the field of Western thought, Buddhism has come to stay.

3

Orthodoxy in Buddhism

Buddhism is unique among the so-called religions of the world in having no criteria for orthodoxy. It has no Pope, no dogmas which must be believed, and no Bible in the Christian sense of inspired revelation. It has no equivalent of Christian baptism, nor can any man be expelled from its fold. In brief, 'A Buddhist is as a Buddhist does'.

Judged by the usual criteria, Buddhism is not a religion at all. The hallmarks of a religion are a personal God, an unchanging and immortal soul, and the necessity for the salvation of the latter by the former. These three factors are entirely absent in Buddhism. The importance of the distinction is that all religions provide an authority, and Buddhism has none. The reported advice of the All-Enlightened One to the Kalamas should never be forgotten. 'Do not be misled by report, or tradition, or hearsay. Do not be misled by proficiency in the Pitakas, nor by mere logic and inference, nor after considering reasons, nor after reflection on some view and approval of it—nor because the recluse (who holds it) is your teacher.'

What, then, is the test? The Scripture points out that when the student knows for *himself* that the teaching is good, and that when applied it conduces to spiritual gain and the elimination of suffering, then, and then only, should it be accepted.

If this is the teaching of the Buddha, those who claim the canon as an absolute authority are in a cleft stick, for the canon itself would seem to be authority for saying that nothing else than personal experience is authority for the individual

Buddhist on the Way. But if the canon is not authority, what is? Why should not anyone claim Rationalism—or for that matter Communism—as good Buddhism, for all have features in common?

The answer is clear though perhaps unpalatable to some; we must distinguish Truth, the teachings of the Buddha, and Buddhism. We do not know what is absolute Truth, and we shall not know until we attain Nirvana; nor do we know precisely what the Buddha taught! We have a written record which, in the course of the two thousand years since it was first written down, has obviously been added to, subtracted from and 'edited'; but when the canon was first written down it had already passed through four hundred years of memorizing, and it is inconceivable, in spite of Indian powers of memory, that that which was written down was precisely that which was heard by those in the presence of the Buddha.

But even if those present at the first great Council understood the Teaching, they could only repeat what they themselves had understood and, great though many of these men were, they were not of the standing of the Buddha's Enlightenment. As for 'Buddhism', this is a Western term for the vast range of varied thought and teaching now to be found in the various parts of the Buddhist world.

Then what is to be taught as Buddhism, in the sense of the teaching of the Buddha? Obviously there must be some form of comparative authority, and obviously the best basis for such teaching is the canon as it now exists. In the Anguttara Nikaya of the Pali Scriptures there is reference to the 'four great authorities' which seem to be placed in diminishing value : the authority of one who hears the Buddha's teaching for himself; that of one who hears the teaching of a gathering of bhikkhus, led by an Elder; the authority of a group of bhikkhus; and finally that of a single bhikkhu, 'an expert in Dhamma'.

This canon as it is taught today by the bhikkhus is rational, coherent as a whole, and sufficient to the needs of a large proportion of mankind. It is a moral-philosophy of immense clarity and power. It is objective in its analysis of the nature of life and, in particular, of the cause of suffering; it is subjective in the Way which it sets out for the removal of the cause. It is above all supremely self-reliant, relying upon no outside power, divine or human, to save the individual from the consequences of his own hatred, lust and illusion. Having no authority for the nature of Truth, it has never persecuted those who differ from a particular point of view, and in its supreme tolerance presents the cleanest record of all the so-called religions of the world.

But is this canon alone entitled to be described as Buddhism? Is the Pali canon Buddhism and Buddhism the Pali canon? To an objective student the answer is clearly 'No'. Long before this canon was written down there were signs of expansion from its limited teaching, and these now include cosmology, mysticism, philosophy, metaphysics, religion, art and culture which between them present the widest and noblest range of thought produced by man. Are all these latter developments outside the pale of Buddhism? Are all these Mahayana schools and sects heretical? And are none of the tens of millions who are members of them entitled to be called Buddhists?

He is a bold man who would answer 'No' to this last question, for all these schools—with the possible exception of the Shin sect of Japan — accept the Thera Vada as the basis of their Buddhism. The Mahayanist might point out that in numbers they are ten times as great as the Theravadins, that their heritage is at least two thousand years old, and that Mahayanist countries have produced some of the greatest minds, some of the greatest literature and some of the greatest art of which the world holds record. If this be true, and any student can verify it for himself, those Theravadins who smugly claim their own particular heritage as commensurate with Buddhism are surely in danger of looking a little foolish?

Where then, when surveying the great field of Buddhism, are we to draw the line as to where orthodoxy, if such there be, should end? The answer will vary with the student. If self-reliance be the very essence of Buddhism, then the Shin sect of Japan is indeed beyond the pale, for it is difficult indeed to see how its teaching is compatible with the whole tenor of the teaching of the Buddha. Again, it has been said that much of Tibetan Buddhism is a long way indeed from the Master's teaching, but who shall say where the line should be drawn? In these difficult circumstances it is easy to appreciate the Sinhalese point of view. This at least, they say, pointing to the Pali canon, is the Dhamma, and we want no more.

But the Western student, in the course of an impersonal survey of the whole field of Buddhism, may find other schools which, though admittedly deriving their teaching from the principles to be found in the Pali canon, have claimed their own extended teaching to be true by the very authority set down in the canon. Millions, they say, in the course of two thousand years, have found for themselves that the Teaching as they have been taught is true.

Buddhism is either alive or dead, and the test of life is the faculty of inner progress. It is true that Truth does not change, but our knowledge and understanding of it and, above all, our application of it to the requirements of the day must change perpetually.

Would the Buddha himself have had it otherwise? Are we the senseless guardians of a dead museum exhibit, or pilgrims marching side by side to our own and the world's enlightenment? Let our Buddhism be that which we have received as the Buddha Dhamma in whatever school and which, on the Eightfold Path to Peace, we have found for ourselves to be true; as such it may yet prove the salvation of mankind.

Basic Buddhism

4

Three Signs of Being

The three Signs of Being are basic to all Buddhism. They are not proffered as doctrine but as fact, and their existence is to be tested by every student for himself before he accepts them. Thereafter it is for him to test the inferences and appropriate action which the Buddha claimed should follow from the fact.

Sabbe sankhara anicca, reads the Pali wording. *Sabbe sankhara dukkha. Sabbe dhamma anatta.* The *sankhara* are compounded things, aggregates, formations, as distinct from elements, if such there be, which cannot be reduced into component parts. Western Science has now reached the Buddhist point of saying that even the atom is infinitely complex, and that the concept of matter may be equated with that of flow. The Signs of Being are therefore these: All 'things' are *anicca,* changing and therefore impermanent; all 'things' are *dukkha,* unhappy, suffering in the sense of being incomplete, imperfect, 'joined to the unloved, separated from the loved'; and all 'things', conditional and unconditional, without exception are *anatta,* without a separate 'soul' or quality of permanence which marks them as eternally distinct from other 'things'.

The list is not fortuitous. The Buddhist regards the Buddha as the holder of the supreme spiritual office in the hierarchy of perfected men. His Teaching, therefore, was not the observations of a thinker who noticed, among other qualities of matter, the signs to which he drew attention. If he emphasized and taught the application of precisely three it is because these three, and their intimate and complex interrelation, form a central position in his teaching.

C

The several Signs and their application are set out in a hundred text-books, as well as again and again in the Pali canon. The purpose of this present survey is to stress the interrelation of the three, a factor which is seldom emphasized. First, however, the nature of the Signs and their central position in the Buddha's Dhamma, or Teaching, must be again made clear.

'All things are changing.' As a statement of fact this is trite. It is scientifically obvious, and as applied to human life is the subject of perennial sermons, poems and sentimental regret. The cycle of form is everywhere apparent. All that we know, visible and invisible, of tangible fact or intangible concept, proves the cycle of birth, growth, decay and death, while the 'life' which used the form moves on. Life is flow, movement. The law of progress, or regress, is a perpetual becoming; it is we who add the epithets of 'better' or 'worse' to the next stage in the process. Karma (Pali: *kamma*) is rightly called the mode of change, for it is the law of cause-effect wherein the change develops as it does and not otherwise. Rebirth is the field of change in time.

To apply the doctrine to the plans and purposes of daily life, to use it to affect and mould ambition, to decide the choice of job and use of income, and to settle the attitude of mind to family and all possessions, this is another matter. To agree that all is in a state of flux is easy, for it is impossible to think of anything to which the law does not apply. But to use the law, to mould habitual thought and enterprise to accord with its cold decree, this is unusual, but worth the effort involved. 'Life is a bridge; pass over it, but build no house upon it.' What admirable advice, but what does it imply? It means that on earth there is no such thing as security, and it is useless to look for it. It means that the wise man uses what Alan Watts has rightly called 'the wisdom of insecurity', and accepts the flow of life as he accepts the law of gravity. Happiness, indeed, begins when we live as if *anicca* were true. In a world of *anicca* there can be no 'authority', human or otherwise. All, all without exception, is changing. There is therefore no such thing as static ownership, for that which owns is changing rapidly, faster probably than that which it claims to own. Even possession is suspect. Do I truly possess some much-loved *objet d'art*? If so, what possesses it? My body, my emotions, my mind? All are changing, and soon the 'I' and the object will alike be very different. Regret for old age, and the passing of this and that, is clearly foolish; so also is the longing for a state of things which has not yet arrived. There is a charming story of an Indian prince who sent for his jeweller and asked him to make a ring with a phrase engraved on it which would sustain him in adversity and abate his pride in moments of success. The jeweller made the ring, and on it the prince read: 'It will pass'. The wise man sees the truth of Kipling's phrase, and when he meets with triumph or disaster 'treats those two impostors just the same'. The wheel turns, and we on the edge of it resist the turning. Yet at the hub there is only Here and Now and This, and change makes no disturbance. At the heart of the tornado there is peace; at the heart of change there is peace, but it only comes to the man who accepts the law and uses it to its own fulfilment.

Dukkha is the converse of sukha, usually translated 'happiness'. To equate it with the extremes of suffering or grief is to distort the teaching in order to evade its power. It has been argued that Buddhism is a philosophy of suffering. But if suffering, in the sense of a feeling of frustration, dissatisfaction, 'union with the unloved and separation from the loved', is true, and capable of proof by any man, then why should it not be emphasized? None can doubt the fact of dukkha and its omnipresence. At a given moment a man may claim to be 'happy', whatever that may mean, but is his neighbour next door happy? And if not, what is the quality of happiness that is indifferent to his neighbour's woe?

Suffering is not an evil but a necessary friend. It teaches error, whether the folly of eating unripe fruit or the futility of self-aggrandizement at the expense of one's fellow men. The wise man, therefore, accepts the fact of suffering and controls his reaction to its advent on each plane—in the body, in the emotions and feelings or in the mind. There are four Noble Truths, said the All-Enlightened One. The first is the omnipresence of dukkha; the second is its cause, self-ishness; the third is the obvious fact, though all too rarely applied, that the way to remove the result is to remove the cause, and the fourth is a detailed description of the means of removing it. This Noble Eightfold Path, the moral code of Buddhism, may be found set out in any Buddhist text-book and is only mentioned here to emphasize that the omnipresence of suffering must be coolly faced before efforts are made to remove it. Only then will the efforts be strenuous, intelligent and maintained.

The recognition of suffering and its cause may be used for the mind's development. But the mind's attempts to escape from suffering are legion in number and infinite in form. We shrink from the dentist, and make more fuss about a sore finger than in our more dispassionate moments we would care to admit. We run from emotional pain. We will not read of that which hurts our pride or fears or 'feelings'. We forget, or gloss over, or excuse, an experience which injured the tentacles of our personality. We forget the psychiatrist's definition of a neurosis as 'refused pain'. In the same way we escape from mental pain. We refuse to believe what we do not like. There are those who say that they do not believe in rebirth because they do not wish to be reborn. Do they equally regret the law of gravity when a slate from a roof falls on their head? We refuse to discuss what we hope is not true, forgetting that hope itself is a form of fear.

The wise man, therefore, accepts the fact of suffering, and its omnipresence and inevitability. He looks for its cause and considers the means for its removal. He finds the cause in self.

The third Sign of Being is *anatta*, which literally means that no 'thing' whatsoever has an *atta* (Sanscrit: *atman*). In view of the gross misapprehension on the meaning of this doctrine, which is basic to all schools of Buddhism, it is important to understand that the Buddha never taught that there is no Self or reincarnating entity; still less did he teach no SELF, in the sense of an Absolute beyond the reach of words. The Buddha taught that in none of the constituents of the personality, the physical body, feelings, mental attributes and discriminative consciousness is there a permanent element which distinguishes that man from any other. What is in common is not the property of any man, any more than the life which informs each daisy in a field is the exclusive possession of that flower. There is life, and it functions or is expressed in infinitely various forms. My neighbour and 'I' are two of them, but though he and I each have a 'Self', in the sense of a reincarnating bundle of attributes or composite character, we do not each possess some 'spark of the Divine' or 'immortal soul' which is his and not mine or mine and not his, eternally. As to the nature of the SELF the Buddha maintained 'a noble silence', for no words can describe the Indescribable.

So much for doctrine, that the self we know is impermanent and, like all other forms, inseparable from suffering; that the nobler Self must learn to dominate, purify and control the self; that whatever SELF there be it is not yours or mine and is by the intellect unknowable. For the rest, as Dr Suzuki puts it, *anatta* is not a matter of doctrine but of experience.

The application of the *anatta* doctrine is of the utmost value in the inner life, and probably distinguishes the Buddhist process of self-deliverance from others. The first step is to realize, make real in daily thought and act, the distinction between the Non-self and the Self. What is it desires and makes decisions, what controls the daily round and life's planning? Is it the selfish, animal, lower side of us, or the compassionate, 'higher' mind? When it is realized that self-ishness, the belief in the ultimate importance of 'I', is an illusion, just a silly idea, an attempt by the part to fight the purpose of the whole, it will be seen that self is the only Devil, the true cause of evil and of most of our suffering.

The Buddhist Way is therefore the process of the death of self. As self dies the Self grows, and as the Self is purified, the light of SELF, the awareness of Enlightenment, grows in the mind which now returns in fullest consciousness to the All-Mind whence it came. This is not doctrine but experience, and there is time enough to ask what moves from life to life, what dies and what lives on within the mystery of Nirvana, when the questioner is far upon the Way. By then he will know, and will not need to ask.

So much for the Signs of Being. What is their true relation? In the Pali canon we find but little help. It is written, 'Material shape is impermanent. What is impermanent is *dukkha*. What is *dukkha* is not Self. What is not my Self that am not I'.[1] Simple reasoning can expand this meagre hint. All things are *anicca*. All beings, and in particular mankind, are *dukkha*. The bridge which links the *anicca* of things to the *dukkha* of man is the

---

[1] *Samyutta Nikaya.* iii. 44-5. Trans. I. B. Horner.

latter's false belief in self, the illusion of separation, the unawareness of Non-duality. While we are in the illusion of *anatta*,
anicca causes us *dukkha*. Remove the illusion and the link is
broken. Thus *anatta* is the prime cause of suffering in that it is
the base in which adheres the desire for self.

Again, all is *anicca*, and man is no exception to the rule.
Anatta is therefore the application of *anicca* to man, in that all
his parts, with no exception whatever, are without permanence
and immortality. But man resents the application of *anicca* to
self, and persists in the pleasant illusion that 'I' am important,
that 'I', whatever my demerits now, will sooner or later achieve,
earned or unearned, my ultimate salvation, to dwell thereafter
in eternal bliss. Because most of our minds are dominated with
self the thought of the end of self is horror, and the self fights
valiantly to preserve its beloved illusion. This fight is the cause
of *dukkha*, for when every unit of life is fighting for self-
preservation, for self-aggrandizement, the reign of *dukkha* is
established and for long assured.

Again, *anicca* is impermanence, the unreality of form. The
implication is that life is One, and uses for its better expression
a million million forms, including, but with no particular
preference, the parts of men. In our ignorance, the *avidya* or
absence of light that fosters the error of self, we claim for self a
separate existence. We act accordingly, and *dukkha* in a
thousand forms is born and again reborn perpetually.

The Signs of Being, therefore, are not fortuitously chosen, and
when the Buddha with his vast, omniscient mind proclaimed
that these were the signs or marks of sentient existence, it was
not that these among others were worth the disciples' attention.
Rather they form a complete philosophy of life, the premises of
which are not delivered as dogma but as facts which each man
could and must find to be true.

5

Soul or No Soul

Buddhism is commonly described as one of the great religions of the world, but it is not in the ordinary sense of the term a religion. It knows no personal yet Absolute God as postulated, for example, by the Christians, and it has no priesthood engaged in the work of that God in the salvation of souls, for it does not admit the existence in man of an 'immortal soul' which it needs a God to save. All this is easily said, and it is at least speciously correct. But it is easy to play with words and concepts in such a way as to mask the spiritual teaching which they strive to embody. In popular consideration Buddhism is one of the great religions of mankind, and the above arguments are usually brushed aside as of no fundamental value. Let us look again, therefore, at the concept of soul.

The nature of the soul and the nature of God, using both these terms in their broadest possible sense, are related concepts. One may approach the truths they enshrine (or distort) either from below, as it were, by reasoning from known premises, or by accepting the direct 'experience' of the thousands of mystics and mighty thinkers a fair number of whom have flowered in the field of Buddhism. The intellectual and mystical approach may be collated with the Jnana and Bhakti Yoga of Indian philosophy, and both, at their higher levels, are suffused with light revealed by the other. Both achieve an awareness of a noumenon behind phenomena which, itself beyond the reach of thought, is to be known in and through its countless manifestations in the relative, visible world. The ways of expressing this dual fact of the

Absolute and Relative, the Unmanifest and Manifest, the Uncreated and the Created, are countless in a hundred tongues. The Buddhist teaching, itself to be found in the Theravada School, is one of the simplest. 'There is O Bhikkhus, an Unborn, Unbecome, Unformed; were it not for this Unborn, Unbecome, Unformed, there could be no escape from birth, becoming. But because there is this Unborn . . . there is an escape from birth . . . '

But the human mind, and above all the highly developed metaphysical mind of India, could never be long content with hints of the Unborn, and the fact that it was manifest in the born, without wanting to know more of the process by which the one became the other, that is, in the terms of our enquiry, how God became man. Nor were the early Buddhists pioneers in this field. There is in existence 'the accumulated wisdom of the ages', tested and verified by generations of Arhats, or whatever name one uses to describe those who achieved the Buddha-wisdom. The Buddha Gautama has been called the 'patron of these Adepts' and as such he might have been expected to add to the sum total of man's awareness of the universe. But he chose to concentrate on proclaiming the Way which leads the individual man beyond his individuality, out of the world of illusion into the light of Enlightenment. The house of self is on fire, he said. Get out of it, and quickly.

All speculation on ultimates, or on the relation between the One and the Many, were relegated by the Buddha to the pigeon-hole of matters 'unprofitable', on the ground that the man who is treading the way to the end of suffering has no time for such things. But Buddhism is now presented to the Western mind, and the Western mind of today likes to be considered scientific. It delights in 'working hypotheses' which progressive tests will prove or disprove, and it is not easily content with mere directions about a Way. True, the thinkers of the West are apt to suffer from the same hiatus between hypothesis and personal application which is common to thinkers in all parts of the world, but their metaphysics are as elaborate as any system in the East. In essence the metaphysics of all peoples consist of an Absolute, which is *ex hypothesi* beyond discussion or description, and which the Indians call THAT. From THAT, the Unnameable, comes the One, which manifests as the primordial duality, the 'pairs of opposites', which in turn can only be understood in conjunction with some relation between them; hence three, the primordial trinity of all religions, and from these three flow the '10,000 things', as the Chinese call the world of Samsara. The life-force which informs and uses these innumerable forms is itself the manifestation of the One—things born are born of the Unborn, in Buddhist parlance—and from this unity of life flows brotherhood as a fact in nature and compassion for all other forms of the one life. The law of karma is made more understandable.

If 'God' is regarded as the highest concept reached by some theistic religions in their climb towards the nameless Absolute, then that which informs all forms, including the muddled mess of characteristics which walk about as men, *is* in a sense the father and creator of those forms, each of which is the child of its preceding conditions ('that arising, this becomes'); and 'the union of man with God' will pass as Buddhist, subject to a much improved description of 'man' and 'God'. If this phrase, or its Buddhist equivalent, is allowed to have no meaning in Buddhist minds then what is Para-nirvana, unless it is indeed beyond the wheel of becoming of the manifested universe? Do Buddhists feel the necessity to quarrel with the 'Thou art THAT' of the Indian philosophy in which the Buddha was born and bred? Is the phrase not right, in the Buddhist Society's 'Twelve Principles of Buddhism'; 'Buddhism does not deny the existence of God or soul, though it places its own meaning on those terms'? By God the Buddhist means THAT from which the universe was born, the Unborn of the Buddhist Scriptures, and by soul that factor in the thing called man which moves towards Enlightenment. Why need more be said of it, at any rate by those who are not content with scholarship, but strive to attain that same Enlightenment?

What, then, of those in the Theravada School who cry by day and night, 'No soul, no soul, no soul', yet in their dealings with their fellow-Buddhists behave at times as those who proclaim a doctrine which they do not believe to be true? It is surely a dreary, joyless and unprofitable doctrine, for if there is nothing to enter Nirvana how can this teaching conduce to peace of mind, to Nirvana, which is the test for all Buddhist teaching? It is rejected by all that we know of the higher avenues of knowledge, and if it be argued that it may be true for all that, let it be realized that *it was never taught by Gautama the Buddha!* Why, then, do so many cling to this negative and dismal teaching, which the essential gaiety and happiness of the peoples of Thailand, Burma and Ceylon, where the Theravada School holds sway, combine to prove untrue? If it is contrary to reason and experience, and not Buddhism, why is it still taught as part of the Way to Enlightenment?

It may be because it is partially true, and contains a new presentation of a tremendous truth, that none of the *skandhas*, the constituent factors of the personality, contain a permanent self or soul, nor do they all together constitute such an entity. This is tremendous teaching, and it is indeed the heart of the Dhamma. Yet not content with this great negative, which the Buddha flatly refused to develop into a complementary positive, members of the Sangha at some point in history took it upon themselves to teach what the Buddha never taught, that there is no quality beyond the *skandhas* which is a reflection or manifestation, call it what one will, of THAT, 'the Unborn', of which the universe as a whole is a partial and perishable expression. That the doctrine so taught by the Theras of today is only partially true is proved by the words of the Pali canon itself. What is the 'Self which is lord of self', of which we read in the Dhammapada, and what is the meaning of all the other distinctions between two 'selves'? Is that which strives by mind-development of every kind, to achieve samadhi and then Nirvana, merely a 'condition-propelled continuum'? If so, it is strange that all the mystics, prophets, saints and the great artists of the ages, many of them products of the Buddhist world, should all be deluded fools.

If Buddha never taught that there is no self, let us in the newly created spirit of world Buddhism cease to teach it. Surely in stressing the unreality of the self which is, as the Buddha proved, the source of all our suffering, we have enough on hand to apply. We need not add the impossible task of proving that that which works for the end of suffering is itself not merely unreal as pertaining to the world of the relative, but not even a fair reflection of the Light of Enlightenment which moves in a million forms, for itself and all that lives towards that full Enlightenment.

Perhaps this is the source of the trouble, that we argue too long on the nature of self, and move too little to that personal and spiritual experience in which alone we shall learn its meaning. Perhaps Dr Suzuki was right when he said that *anatta* was not a doctrine but a matter of experience. Meanwhile, whether we call this compound, changing bundle of characteristics 'soul' or 'Self' seems to matter little so long as it moves unceasingly to something better, nearer to the heart's desire of the final Awakening. To the extent that it is of the Absolute, as all in manifestation must be part, it is not mine; I have no immortal soul. To the extent that any self is mine and speaks through the voice of 'I' it is not immortal. If the Buddhists say, 'Kill self and the Light will shine', and the Christians say, 'Kill self, and your soul will be united again with God', are they fighting on fundamentals, or on the means of expressing an experience which none can properly describe?

Let us then go forward to become what in essence we are, *buddha*, 'awakened'. It is worthy of note that no Mahayanist, of any of its schools, accepts the monk-made teaching of the Theravada School upon this point, although the teaching of Sunyata has been described as the *anatta* doctrine to the nth degree. Yet the Mahayana has produced some of the world's greatest art, some of its noblest thinking, and some of its greatest minds. Perhaps their common factor was an awareness that life *is* one, and that it is an expression of the UNCREATE. If so, then surely he who cries 'No self, no self', and means no self at all, no growing self beyond the limits of our low desires and clouded minds, will find no happiness and no release, not even for himself, much less for all mankind.

6

The Threefold Self

Self is the theme of all religions, and enters into all departments of human thought. In Buddhism it is central and paramount, for the goal of the Buddhist Path is Enlightenment, the enlightenment of something which, for want of a better name, I will here call Self. Just what this is, and is not, is debated in all schools of Buddhism.

When I first discovered Buddhism I read much of 'No self, No self', so I naturally enquired, 'What is it, then, that treads the Path that leads to the end of suffering?' What is this force or power which, at various levels of consciousness, uses me, or I am, or I am told to 'drop' as illusion? I have heard no answer. As against this, in my reading in comparative religion I found the 'Spirit, soul and body' of St Paul most helpful, and I still do. Of all analyses, from the sevenfold of esoteric Yoga to the five *skandhas* of Theravada Buddhism and the Buddha's 'Noble silence' as to what lay beyond, this three-fold division, which I have there called SELF, Self and self, seemed the simplest and most useful. But a fellow student, while agreeing its utility, enquired of its authority in Buddhist text. I replied that as a good Buddhist I do not rely on authority, but I agree that I should try to show that what I have found to be true can fairly be described as Buddhism, though not necessarily in so many words in any one school.

Let us consider the three terms.

Spirit is one of a hundred names for the Indescribable. The Buddha called it 'the Unborn, Unoriginated, Uncreated,

Unformed'. The Mahayana speaks of the Dharmakaya, the Dharma-body or Dharma incarnate and, in another school, Alayavijnana, the 'Store-consciousness' or absolute Unconscious. In the famous literature of the 'Wisdom that has gone beyond' it is referred to as Sunyata, Emptiness or the Void (of all distinction or separateness). Buddhist mystics speak of the Buddha within, as in *The Voice of the Silence*—'Look within, thou art Buddha'. In Zen Buddhism it is described as the beyond of thinking—hence 'No-mind'. Lao-tzu called it Tao, a term as untranslatable as Dharma; Eckhart spoke of God-head beyond God, that from which God came; the Hindus call it THAT. It is absolute, compared with the ever-changing, ever-becoming flux of Samsara, the manifested universe, and though 'interdiffused' in every 'thing' it remains absolute. In Christian terms, it is at the same time utterly transcendent and completely immanent. Every thing, seen and unseen, from a neutron to a universe, is alive with *tathata*, suchness, that which makes that thing precisely what it is and not otherwise, but the suchness is the same in each. And every thing is every other thing in the 'unimpeded interdiffusion of all particulars (Jijimuge) as described in the Kegon school of Japanese Buddhism. As for man's relation to this Unborn Absolute of Spirit, the Hindus have expressed it in three words—'Thou art THAT', for they say of the universe, 'There is THAT (*Paramatman*, the SELF). There is nothing else.' Are they wrong?

In human terms, Nirvana is a state of consciousness in which all sense of separation, of difference, is dissolved. Here is the ultimate mystery, that the unit of consciousness, freed of illusion, having shed the last vestige of a separate self, is free, and knows that it is free. As a drop in the ocean of THAT, the 'Unborn', it knows itself, the drop, to be the ocean. The prodigal son has returned to his father's home. 'Thou art (again) THAT.' 'I and my Father are one.'

So much for Spirit, which is never mine, never yours; it is beyond the reach and range of Scripture, which is, as written down, but the product of the human mind. It *is*; it is no 'thing', and the universe is but its partial expression, 'breathed out' as the Hindus say, for the vast period of a Maha-manvantara, and then breathed in for a period of rest as long.

45

Body lies at the other extreme, the opposite pole of being, and is the easiest to understand. *Rupa,* form or body, is the lowest of the five *skandhas* of Pali Buddhism, and to this may be added the persona or mask through which we are known to our fellow humans. This personality is the vehicle for that strange illusion which besets us all, the ego or self, which need not, however, be 'destroyed'; it is enough to observe, with newly opened eyes, that it just does not exist! This awareness comes but slowly on the long journey to the mind's enlightenment for, as I have written elsewhere, it is easy to say of the self, 'Just drop it', but it needs great courage and, for most of us, long training to 'let go'.

But Spirit and Body, SELF and self, are two extremes, the balancing opposites in a bi-polar field. The concept of duality is sterile. Twoness alone is static; it is the relationship between the two that causes *bhavana,* becoming, becoming more until that which is achieving more becomes the Most. Clearly something lies between ultimate Spirit and the gross illusion of the ego-self encased in its one-life body. What is it that is bound upon the Wheel and struggles to be free? What creates and suffers karma, learns that all is suffering and, accepting from the Buddha that its cause is *trishna,* base desire, sets out to remove it? To what in whom was the Buddha speaking when he exhorted those about him with his dying breath to 'work out your salvation with diligence', if not to the Self that is or should be 'Lord of self', as described in the Dhammapada?

It is clearly more than Body, more than the ego which in the noblest minds has largely ceased to exist. It lies behind and beyond the personality, and may by comparison be called the individual. But equally it is less than the 'unborn' Spirit, for its complex, ever-evolving mess of ingredients is sadly imperfect in all the humans that we know. I regard it as the 'Soul' of St Paul and I have called it for convenience Self.

Of course it is illusion, judged in the light of Spirit; so is all manifestation. Of course it is subject to the three Signs of Being, change, suffering and *anatta,* in the sense of having no unchanging principle which divides it from all in being. Of course it burns with the Three Fires of hatred, lust and illusion. But to argue, with or without a volume of technical terms from the Abhidhamma, that it just does not exist seemed to me forty years ago and seems to me now plain silly. It ex-ists, as a thing in manifestation, as much as hatred, a headache or the Brighton Pier.

What is it? I dislike definitions, for they shut up a ray of truth in a box of words. But whether described as 'a discrete continuum of karmic impulse' or the reincarnating entity, it is what it is and should be used as such. It is certainly complex, for it contains four of the five *skandhas,* together with imagination, memory, base and noble thinking, and the intuition at the highest yet achieved. It likewise contains, and in a sense *is* the whole mass of its unexpended karma, whether 'good', as of the six noble virtues, or 'bad' as of the numberless defilements to which the mind is heir. And all this is in a constant state of flux, with ever-shifting interrelation and inter-causation of its parts and principles, as set out in the Twelve Nidanas. It grows in each life with the new body which its own karma attracted it to use, and begins to influence and be influenced by all with whom it comes in contact in thought, word and deed. It is therefore not 'an immortal soul', as the phrase is used in Christianity, and the pioneers of Buddhism in Europe were right to reject the word soul from Buddhist literature. But the thing which I call Self exists in all of us, and will continue to exist until that thing or individual merges in Nirvana. Until that day it will be lit from above by Spirit, held down in ignorance by the low desires of self, and be fighting, splendidly or feebly, to regain the full awareness of the Buddha-mind within.

It is surely therefore unwise to over-stress 'No-self, No-soul' in modern Buddhist literature, for the man in the street who meets this in his first essay in Buddhism is apt to remark that 'this is demonstrably untrue'. And the Buddha never said it, though apparently pressed to do so. He merely said that the *skandhas* and all 'things' are devoid of an abiding self, a magnificent teaching which every human being badly needs. For the rest he maintained 'a noble silence', for he could not say that the Unborn, Unoriginated, Unformed did or did not 'exist'. Both statements are true, and neither.

Buddhism, then, rejects emphatically the concept of an immortal soul, as something which for ever distinguishes any 'Self' from any other. But to say that each of us is the Unborn encased for a while in *avidya*, ignorance, is in a mystical sense true.

Meanwhile the battle rages, for the Self, as it moves from birth to birth, through aeons of time which appal our Western minds with their immensity, is a battlefield of low desire and spiritual aspiration, in which the higher mind, striving towards a clearly perceived ideal, deplores the ego's base activities. As St Paul himself observed for all of us, 'For the good that I would I do not; but the evil which I would not, that I do.' Yet we have no cause for complaint. 'Master, how shall I be free?' asked a pupil. Said the master, 'Who puts you under restraint?' For this Self or 'soul', as the Theravadins, Mahayanists and Zen masters alike insist, is itself in the end seen as illusion, a cloud passing over the sun of Spirit, or, as the Diamond Sutra has it, 'a star at dawn, a bubble in a stream, a flickering lamp, a phantom and a dream'. But to say that it does not exist is, in my experience, bad philosophy, bad Buddhism and bad sense. For it does 'ex-ist' in the precise meaning of that term, that, like the universe, it stands out, has come forth, been born from the Unborn. So does a bubble exist for a while, having been born or caused, but shortly to cease to ex-ist. The cry of 'No self', therefore, is unwise. There is a Self, each with its shadow self, but each is no more immortal than a butterfly.

To the mystic all this is obvious. For him only the Buddha within is real; the rest, the whole of it, is a mode of the Absolute which is but relative and will, when time is not, disappear.

The Self, then, the complex bundle of characteristics which may be called character, is not to be confused with Spirit, but is more real, if the term be permitted, than self. Consciousness, the No-mind of the Unborn in manifestation, can function, it seems, on what plane it will. In a hot bath we are purely physical; in a burst of affection higher than that. In the concrete mind we use an impersonal instrument; in the heights of intellect a God-like power; and with the intuition the SELF perceives itself as one and indivisible. Most of us live habitually at the level of lower mind as motivated by personal desire, yet reach at times to nobler levels of thinking. In my chosen terms, for most of the time we are Self. For too much of it we are down in the self; for too little of it we are aware of that which is alone Reality, the

Unborn SELF, in which distinctions of all kinds have ceased to be.

Is all this academic, playing with words? Not for me. I have found it helpful for some forty years. I am aware every minute of the Buddha-principle alive and shining in every 'thing', including me, and no distinction between them. I can at times lift consciousness to be more aware of it and to see my fellow beings, each an aspect of the SELF in Self in self, as equally bound in karma and equally struggling to be free. I am also aware of the ego-self still very much alive within me, its pride and arrogance feeding the fires of hatred and lust and illusion. But while I accept this part of the total entity which for this cycle of illusion bears my name I refuse to be bound by it. Gradually I progress on the Path and at times see 'suddenly' a flicker of the light of Spirit, the Unborn sole Reality. I know of no one utterly spiritual, no one utterly base. If it is difficult to see the Spirit in the lowest type of habitual criminal I know that the light is there, that all things are imbued with the same 'suchness' and come, as the Buddha said, from the same Unborn.

I may be reminded that 'all distinctions are falsely imagined', but for working purposes I have found this threefold division helpful in understanding myself and my fellow men. As the Dhammapada points out, 'Self is the lord of self and the goal of self'. When this lordship is established and recognized we shall each be that much nearer to the SELF which we have never ceased to be.

7

Self and Suffering

Before leaving the Signs of Being, which I regard as fundamental to Buddhist Teaching and worthy of far more study than is usually accorded them, let us look again at their relationship and particularly at that between the false belief in self and the believer's suffering. 'This do I teach,' said the Buddha, 'suffering and the end of suffering', and the famous Four Noble Truths—the omnipresence of suffering, its cause, the fact that the cause may be removed, and the Way to its utter ceasing—these are at the heart of Buddhism in all its schools. And the cause of suffering, said the Buddha, lies in the doctrine of *anatta*.

The average man admits the existence of suffering, for he cannot ignore it; but he does his best to keep it from his mind, and if religion insists on its recognition he firmly imputes it to the will of God even though he cannot explain why God, who is Good, permits evil. In the same way the Western mind admits that selfishness is a blemish in character, but continues to act on the assumption that the one reality in life is that which grasps all it wants in the name of 'I'! Buddhism teaches otherwise: that every thing, and 'thingness' itself, is inseparable from suffering in some form, and that the false, ingrained illusion of 'I'-ness is the cause of the greater part of it.

Let us look again, then, at the SELF, the Self and the self, for it is idle to deny this trinity. As Dr Evans-Wentz says:

'Unenlightened man, being far from the Full Awakening, believes himself to be possessed of an individualized mind uniquely his own; and this illusion-based belief has given rise to the doctrine of soul. But the Tibetan Teachers declare that the One Cosmic Mind alone is unique; that, on each of the incalculable myriads of life-bearing orbs throughout space, the One Cosmic Mind is differentiated only illusorily, by means of a reflected, or subsidiary, mind appropriate to, and common to, all living things thereon, as on the planet Earth.'[1]

And this Tibetan teaching is basic to the whole field of Mahayana Buddhism.

The SELF, or One Mind, or Absolute, changes in form from the ONE to Two, from Two to Three, and from Three to the Infinite Many. Yet the One and the Many are ONE, and never cease to be so, a fact which is the basis of all mysticism, Buddhist and otherwise, as of all compassion. Each part of this stupendous Whole is an essential part of the Whole, and partakes of the wholeness. As the Whole would not be Whole without each part, each part is, in a super-rational sense, itself the Whole. To this extent each part, and here we are speaking of 'you' and 'me', is a 'divine soul'. Can we not rightly say, then, that somewhere within us is a divine soul which is my soul and your soul respectively? No, says the Buddhist, very much no. If the distinction is subtle it is profound and basic. Every drop of the ocean is wet, but is the drop immortal, and does it own the wetness? Each lamp shines in the room with electricity, but does it own the electricity with which it shines? You and I are alive with the same Life; we do not own it. It uses us, as forms of its expression; then it kills us, as forms, and passes on to new forms of expression. In brief, that in me which is of the One is not mine; that which is 'mine' is fleeting, perishable, suffering, and of the Many.

The Buddha never said, 'There is no self'. Indeed, he most expressly refused to say any such thing. What he did say is that certain specific things are not the Self, being subject to change and suffering. These are the five *skandhas* of physical body, feeling, perception, mental conformation and consciousness. But when the self as we know it is thus taken to pieces and analyzed, what is left to say, 'I'? Only Mind-Only, functioning through the intuition, the faculty in every mind by which that Self or

[1] *The Tibetan Book of the Great Liberation*, p. 12.

awareness of Wholeness contacts and is aware of the Whole. By this alone man moves to Enlightenment; without it the part could never rebecome the Whole.

Each self is an illusion, and the illusion must be purged from that 'Higher Self' which consciously moves on to its own and the world's Enlightenment. Miss I. B. Horner has collected seventeen references to this natural duality within each mind in the Pali Scriptures,[1] the most famous of which, perhaps, is that in the *Dhammapada*:

'Self is the lord of self. What other lord could there be? With self well tamed one gains a lord which is hard to gain.'

But the selflessness of all things, carried to its logical extreme, produces the doctrine of *Sunyata*, the Voidness of all manifestation, and this Void, bereft of attributes, is the One-mind which is the first fruits of the Absolute.

Now let us look again at suffering. Suffering, like self, was born when the One became Two, when God limited himself in order to be God. For when God held up a mirror wherein to see himself and to know that he was God he became Two, not One, and yet the mirror, too, was God. But the mirror, believing itself to be the Whole, fell into the illusion of believing itself to have its own particular Wholeness of a soul, and all the rest of us are subject to the same illusion. There is in fact no such thing as self; only SELF or the 'Essence of Mind', and all its aspects sharing it.

The *anatta* doctrine, then, is not only a statement of fact but obvious. Why, then, do we not live accordingly? Because the self in which we have been trained to believe has grown very powerful, and like all parasites has no desire to be slain. Yet it causes most of our unhappiness. Look again at the doctrine of suffering (*dukkha*). All *sankharas* (aggregates, compound things as distinct from the Indivisible) are *dukkha*, i.e. filled with and inseparable from suffering, whether as actual pain, or in the emotional sense of lust, or hate or fear, or as incompleteness, imperfection in the mind. None doubts it, and if it is true it is not pessimistic but intelligent to face it. Said the Buddha: 'As the sea has one savour, salt, so my Teaching has one savour,

[1] *The Middle Way*, Vol. 27, pp. 77-9.

deliverance from suffering.' Suffering and deliverance from suffering—deliverance by removing self.

Let us face it, perhaps for the first time. First, metaphysically, for as already pointed out, suffering was born with the universe, and only in the awareness of Non-dualism will suffering end. In daily life it is all around us. On the physical plane, it appears as illness and injury of body, limitation of expression, a lack in a thousand forms in the body's circumstance. It appears as fear and hate and desire, three brothers who camp extensively, and with some degree of comfortable welcome, in our minds. In our thinking minds, it appears as ignorance and narrowness of viewpoint and a general sense of inferiority. And even in the spiritual sphere there is the awareness of a Light above us that we cannot reach.

What do we do about it? The Buddhist approach is to suffer it—not nearly as simple as it sounds. Yet the word 'suffer' means to bear, to endure, and hence to 'take' it—if need be on the chin. There should be a genuine acceptance of suffering as a fact inseparable from life. But here the illusion of self, in the sense that self is an illusion, divides our attitude to the suffering we are learning to accept. Our own pain we just suffer, learning to remove the constant cause of it, the desire of self for self. But others' suffering is more and more our personal concern, and it is a fact to be faced that as we climb the ladder of Self-expansion and self-elimination we suffer not less but more. For, as we increasingly become aware of the One Life breathing in each brother form of life we learn the meaning of compassion, which literally means to 'suffer with'. Henceforth the suffering of all mankind is daily ours, and as the sense of oneness grows so does the awareness of 'that mighty sea of sorrow formed of the tears of men'. Here is the glory of the Bodhisattva ideal, to turn aside at the entrance of Nirvana, and to postpone that ultimate guerdon of a thousand lives of effort 'until each blade of grass has entered into Enlightenment'.

But note that the awakening of the Buddha-heart that feels in its own suffering that of all mankind comes when the self that thought of itself alone is dead. Compassion wakens when the drug of selfishness has been purged from the system. Only then can the suffering of others be seen dispassionately in the full extent of its nature, and in the simple nature of its cause. The self is utterly self-ish, striving for itself oblivious of the needs of other selves and of the Whole. It is like a swimmer who swims upstream. For a while his strength will fight the current; in the end the current, the will of the river, will prevail. Such suffering by the part that fights the Whole explains the suffering of the part and provides a criterion for right action. That which serves the Whole is good, and that which opposes it is evil.

Thus self and suffering are inseparable, and the heart's release is to remove the pair of them. How, then, do we slay the self? First by watching it at work, and this is the province of 'mindfulness'. Then, by analyzing its desires and the futility of their achievement. It has been often said that the trouble about desire is that one achieves it, and then there are ashes in the mouth indeed. Compare 'the strength of no desire', and watch it in operation. Who is the strongest man in any gathering convened to effect a common purpose? The man who has no axe to grind, who wants nothing. Then, self must be allowed to die, that the total Self within may raise its head increasingly and in the round of vast endeavour know itself again as One. Meanwhile we suffer from the illusion of our self-hood. To remove the cause we must tread that Middle Way which leads to the end of self, and hence to the end of the suffering of self. Compassion, the will to end all others' suffering, will die with the need of it.

Suffering

To suffer is to suffer well, to accept
The untoward circumstance, to bear with skill
The weighted balance which the fool, inept
In equilibrium, would strive to kill
With flight or malediction. Would he thrust
With hand of will the pendulum of rule
From powered harmony, the law is just
And swings upon the wise man as the fool.
To receive, to suffer wholly, to digest
The living deed's implicit consequence,
Here's error's absolution; full confessed
The deed dies in the arms of immanence.
To suffer is to grow, to understand.
The void of darkness holds a proffered hand.

8

The Use and Abuse of Desire

All men know desire, and in all there is a tension between rival aspects of the mind. In a famous phrase already quoted, St Paul expressed the internal warfare admirably when he said, 'For the good that I would I do not, but the evil which I would not, that I do.'

But the Buddhist is a moral scientist; to all such problems, every form of tension, he applies the scientist's objective, cold enquiry, and in the field of desire asks, what is its nature, its cause and cure?

Desire is concerned with a negative; we desire what we do not have. What we have we may not like, but we no longer desire it. What then, is covered by the term 'desire'? A distinction must at once be made between need and want, and in the science of 'character-building' the difference is profound. The body has needs, such as food and shelter, but all manner of wants arise therefrom which are less legitimate. Sex is a biological necessity for the continuation of the race; when it is exercised in terms of lust for sensual gratification it is no longer a need but has become a want, the satisfaction of which is a hindrance to the mind's expansion towards enlightenment. The same applies to greed for food and wine, or the drug addiction of smoking. The emotions, too, have needs and wants. The need is for expression, and repressed emotion will find an abnormal outlet. Its wants are for violent stimulus. We get a 'kick' out of violence, sex and all 'sensation', whether in real life or at second-hand from the press and the screen. The mind itself has needs and wants, but its composition is so subtle and its parts so intertwined that it is hard to define the difference.

But in every want which is not a legitimate need, judged by the place in evolution of the entity concerned, there is the element of insufficiency, of more or less conscious lack. Yet this inner void, this sense of incompletion is the very antithesis of the genuine *Sunyata*, the Void which is a Plenum-Void, being the fullness of the whole wherein all parts have ceased to clamour for themselves. Desire is in fact a burden to be let fall, a debt to be paid, an obstruction on the way, a cloud in the light of the sun, a serious weakness which, till overcome, may prove the individual's undoing. It is therefore of prime importance to discover what it is that desires.

The self of man is complex, for it exists at every point of the line between its poles of ultimate unity and utter diversity. The polarity is essential to all manifested things, and the tension between the poles is equally necessary. At the 'top' is SELF; at the 'bottom' is self, and the Self, the aspiring bundle of thought, emotion, prejudice and karmic sediment we know as character, moves slowly upward, life after life, from the darkness of *avidya* to the Light of Enlightenment. It follows that desire is in quality various, from the utterly and, for human beings, at all times 'wrong' desire to the ever 'right' desire for enlightenment. To damn all desire as evil is therefore foolish, for without at least one form of it, the urgent will to liberation, there will be no entering on the Way.

Desire may be direct or it may be a substitute for some more subtle and concealed ambition. Thus the craving for drink may conceal a desire to forget an experience which causes pain in its remembrance, and a desire to help one's fellow men by fine philanthropy may mask ambition for the plaudits of one's friends as food for pride.

As desire functions at all stages from utter selfishness to utter selflessness it is important to discover what part of self or Self desires this particular thing. What in me wants to have, or do, or become this thing? When I 'want' a holiday, or another job, or to help my neighbour what in me wants? This question is close allied to motive, of which it has been said there are three levels or planes. First comes the awareness that it pays to do good and does not pay to do evil. Then comes the awakening of *bodhicitta*, the 'wisdom-heart' of compassion, based on the oneness of all life. Finally comes the transcending of all motive, when the right thing is done without thought or purpose, and the final 'purposelessness' is attained. Meanwhile it is wise to assume in oneself the worst, and in others the best of motives. In ourselves we shall probably be right to assume base metal in the noblest thought; we shall help our neighbours to nobility by praising them for doing what they should have done.

In ourselves it is essential to be scientific in an utterly objective analysis of thought-desire. What is it wants? The body, the emotions, the intellect, the flowering of compassion? If the answer seems to be, the will to Enlightenment, how strong is this desire that we describe as will? Do we really want release from the Wheel, the end of suffering for ourselves and all mankind? Do we really crave for the final Goal, as much as a man whose head is held under water craves for air? How much do we want Enlightenment, and how much are we prepared to pay for it? A trifle of our income and convenience, or life, the life of self, itself? The Buddha spoke of the self as a house on fire, from which the wise man would escape with the whole strength of his energy and speed. Are we striving to escape from the cause of suffering, or making only such attempt as does not seriously interfere with our bodily and mental convenience?

If the analysis of want is thorough the student will, in due course, classify himself as on the Arhat or the Bodhisattva path. The difference, as between the two main schools of Buddhism, is historic in terms of development; psychologically, the relative stress is complementary and neither is more 'right' than male is 'better' than female. The Arhat desires liberation from the Wheel and begins with the elimination of low desire in his own mind. The Bodhisattva desires the same, but begins with the salvation, that is, the assistance to liberation, of all mankind. No man is utterly balanced between the comparative emphasis, any more than, as Jung points out, any human being is perfectly balanced between intellectual and emotional development.

We have so far spoken of desire as a craving for that which

we have not got. But the negative aspect is quite as powerful. Even as gravity is rightly spoken of as half a law, in that its opposite, the law of repulsion, is equally powerful, so hatred, and all forms of deliberate separation, discrimination and sense of otherness is only desire in a negative form. 'Union with the unpleasant is painful, painful is separation from the pleasant', said the Buddha, and the negative forms of desire, such as fear and hate, are quite as potent in the cause of suffering as actual craving. When we want, we are jealous of those who have what we want, and envy is a form of hate. We fear what we think may hurt us in our want, and hate accordingly. We run towards what we want, and reach out for it. We run as fast and as far away from what we hate or fear.

What is the purport of this analysis, and what is its value in the daily round? It is this, that desire is the cause of suffering. Such is the profound discovery of Gautama the Buddha, the Enlightened One, and as this discovery forms the main incentive to the Way, it is, from the viewpoint of the individual, the basic truth in Buddhism. If selfishness, the craving of the 'I' for self, is indeed the cause of at any rate the greater part of human suffering, what can be more important than the elimination of that desire? To kill out suffering we must remove its cause; so much is obvious. And is there a better way to eliminate the cause than to destroy the self in which that desire inheres? Is it not best to kill out suffering by killing that which causes its cause, the self and its loud 'per-sona'?

How does self cause the desire which causes suffering? The answer is clear; by the illusion of separateness, the unawareness of One. I crave for what I want, not knowing that there is no I except the total Unity. All that believes that it exists in separation is illusion. There is no 'immortal soul' in man or in the universe. All things, great and small, are equally without a permanent self which separates them from the Life which, in a million million forms, is One Life through the illusion of time we call eternity.

The concept of Oneness, of an indivisible and ultimate Reality, can only be a concept until it is realized, made real, by the direct experience of which such terms as conversion, *satori* and enlightenment are partial expressions. From the viewpoint of a practical moral philosophy of life, and such is Buddhism, it is that by which I intuitively know that I *am*, but have not yet *become*. Unaware that there is no separate I, but only the All-I which is not any I, the part strives to its own advantage, indifferent to the fact that where it succeeds it robs and therefore injures the rest of the total I.

The process of liberation may be viewed negatively, by a successive diminution of the egotism which desires to expand itself to the detriment of all other selves, or positively, in the progressive expansion of the higher centres of awareness into a mystical sense of unity with all that lives. All men serve self, it has been said, but their place in spiritual evolution depends on the size of the self they serve. Is it self, or family, or nation or all mankind?

Unaware of the Oneness of all 'things', or manifested aggregates, men live in the illusion of the opposites, between the two poles of Yin and Yang which make up the field wherein the intellect holds sway. Not knowing Prajna, the unitive Wisdom which shines in all plurality and informs the Plenum-Void of the manifested universe, men strive, singly and in groups, for their several advantage. Nations make war over possession of a plot of land; war-lords, political parties, classes, business combines; Church and State make war; neighbours wanting different things make war; 'I' want the best seat, the best hat at the sales, the best job, the largest chocolate . . .

Quite often I get it. If still completely blinded by the desire for self-aggrandizement there may be a sense of satisfaction, yet somewhere in the deeps of mind is the seed of doubt. There is such a thing as the misery of satisfaction, when the desire was selfish, and some other aspect of the Whole was injured or diminished by the self's success. What possesses the wealth, or job, or honour but the personality—which dies irrevocably at the body's death? The possessions are themselves ephemeral, but that which triumphantly possesses them is far more fleeting. Consciousness is changing faster than the speed of light, and that which boasts of what it owns never existed for two breaths in succession.

Progress, therefore, consists of giving away. Generosity of gift is not enough, though it is a good beginning. For even when the sole possession is in the compass of one room each object in that room may be the subject of such clinging as binds the possessor with the chains of longing to each several thing. Compassion, and the appropriate action, is a higher stage of dispossession. 'There is no such thing as sacrifice; there is only opportunity to serve . . . ' Thereafter comes the spiritual 'poverty' of no more clinging, the total surrender of fear and pride, until there is utter willingness to flow on the tide of becoming, as an integral, contented part of an unimaginable Whole. Thereafter we find that we have what we have given away. 'Give up thy life if thou wouldst live' becomes an understood commandment. We have what we no longer want to have; we grow as we grow less. Our remaining desires are found to be limitations. What a nuisance is the friend who must have this and that, whose likes and hates are infinite, with bitter and loud voiced complaint about the whole of circumstance? How pleasant are the truly great who, wanting nothing, are content with anything. Accepting all things in a world of illusion as born of cause-effect they live in a mind above the opposites, and we call them great because they do so.

Before we can be extraordinary we must be content to be extra ordinary, dropping the upward thrust of self to be noticed in the world of men. Filled with the flatulence of pride, with a wealth of feelings which must not be hurt, we fear the pin which, with a devastating pop, will burst our self-importance. The enlightened mind, on the other hand, cannot be touched by circumstance, and he who begins to grow in spirit learns the unconquerable strength of no desire.

Desire, then, must be raised, ennobled, purified. Meanwhile its lower aspects must be at least controlled. But should desire be fought on its own plane, or is this psychologically futile? Which is better, to fight our lower desire with high desire on the field of the opposites, in a world of duality, or to raise the habitual consciousness above the battlefield, to a plane of awareness where high and low have no more meaning? When the self which desires is dead, as a fire dies out for want of fuelling, there will be no more sense of separation, no more desire for the part to achieve at the expense of the whole. 'Seek ye first the kingdom of heaven . . . ' Why not *begin* with Enlightenment?

This is nonsense, in that it is non-sense. But it may be true, and all who achieve Enlightenment would seem to have found it so.

The key, then, to the problem of desire and the suffering which self-ishness, the desire of self for self, inevitably breeds, is in that faculty of mind which knows, directly and immediately, that the sense of self is illusion. So shall we learn to eschew the least form of desire; even the desire to be free from the desire for no desire . . .

9

The War is Within

Wars arrive because we will them to arrive, and for no other reason. Once war comes it is the state of science at the time which decides whether the weapons used are bows and arrows or bombs. The effects of the declaration of war may differ; the causes are the same.

The will to violence which causes war, the desire to dominate the thoughts and acts of others is, in the minds of those who generate it, partly conscious, partly subconscious and largely unconscious; in the last case all the more potent for being unrecognized.

Those who consciously cause war for the sake of the spoils of war are evil men, and the name of Hitler, for example, will be reviled as evil while men have memory of World War II. It is common sense that those who lead the Services, and earn their preferment and reward by success in that leadership, cannot, to say the least, be entirely averse to war. The same applies to the aggressive type of politician whose foreign policy, when opposition to his country's will is encountered, is one of violence. Though he speaks, and loudly speaks of peace, he is causing war. In these cases, because this type of individual is seldom noted for introspective examination of motive, it is charitable to describe his will to war as subconscious only. The effect is of course the same.

In the third category are found the larger proportion of mankind, particularly the Western variety. Wars are declared by the few; the decision reflects the unconscious will of the many. The larger groups within the state bring pressure on the Government concerned, either loudly or silently. The several political parties, the trade unions, the financial and 'big business' houses, the press, which at once arouses and reflects what is euphemistically described as public opinion but which is in fact mass emotion, all these together press the Government, of course in the name of Peace, Honour and the Brotherhood of man, to declare war. And in what do these units consist save in smaller and smaller groups and families, and in the end, the individual man and woman?

But each individual man who strives for self-aggrandizement, who grasps for himself as much as he can of commodities, such as money, power and honours, which he knows to be in short supply; all who, in such competition as involves the financial if not the physical death of the loser, nevertheless compete for their several advantage; every one of the thrusters for place, in traffic, politics or trade, whose attitude, unexpressed but fiercely concentrated is, 'I am the better man, and the loser . . . well for him it's just too bad', each and every one of these is the cause of war, and collectively will cause it.

True, some forms of ambition, some will to succeed, is laudable in popular morality, is 'reasonable' and even 'right'. But collectively it causes war, by bows and arrows or the H-bomb as the case may be.

For the cause of suffering, said Gautama the Buddha, the All-Enlightened One, is tanha, desire for self, the grasping, craving cry of 'I want this and I want that'. And the craver gets what he wants, for such is the law of cause-effect which scientists declare to be a law of science, and Jesus—'As ye sow so shall ye reap'—declared to be a law of man. And what he wants, however he may deny it, is war. In English law a man is presumed to intend the reasonable consequences of his acts.

If a million men each want what the other wants, and see no reason why they should not have it despite the claims of all others, what must happen? If the government of a hundred million men wants the property of another government of another hundred million men and the mass emotion of the many, fostered by politicians and the press, submerges the cooler reason of the few, the result is war, whether the weapons used are bows and arrows or the H-bomb.

And the cause of the cause? The force behind the blind and urgent selfishness which causes war? Is ignorance, or philosophically Ignorance, the unawareness of the simple fact that Life is one though its forms are multiple, and that men are brothers whether they behave as members of one family or as homicidal and deluded fools. When a man is under the delusion that his self is separate from all other selves, and in some way better, so that his desire must in every disputed cause prevail, is it surprising that larger units, moving in the same fog of illusion, act in concert as an emotionally retarded small boy a million times his natural size?

Life is one, said the Buddha, and the Middle Way to the end of suffering in all its forms is that which leads to the end of the illusion of separation, which enables a man to see, as a fact as clear as sunlight, that all mankind, and all other forms in manifestation are one unit, the infinitely variable appearances of an indivisible Whole. The few who possess the vision shared by the mystics, the poets, the saints and the nobler-minded of all ages, see that this is so, and advocate that life, individual, national and international, should be lived accordingly. These are the minds that founded the League of Nations, the United Nations and all other organizations, large and small, that move to a better awareness of the central Truth on which all science, religion and philosophy is founded. But they preach on a false assumption, that even those men who in mind agree with them will in act and deed apply the truth when seen.

For the war is a war within, and it will not cease until that day when every living thing is gathered back into the Oneness which is beyond all name or human understanding.

In every mind is the battlefield of self versus Self, of the blinded part which fights against the less-deluded flame of the Light which must in time, itself a form of illusion, return enlightened to the Light from which it came. Meanwhile, we live in difference. All religions are not the same, nor all philosophies, and it is a howling lie though a noble one to declare that men are equal. They are in fact infinitely variable, each treading his own path to the mountain top of selflessness, where the vision and the will of oneness are father to the selfless act, and the individual knows first hand 'the strength of no desire'.

Applied, this is a depressing truth, for it means that war is inevitable as long as men want war, and at present nine-tenths of them are busy wanting it. But there are signs of a nobler vision, and it matters not for the moment if the cause of the non-declaration of war be the fear of the ghastly weapons in the enemy's hands, or the love begotten of a sense of unity which one day will alone make war impossible. Let the first for the moment prevail; in the end I believe it will be the second.

Meanwhile, each one of us is hard at war—within. We must face this battlefield; withdraw, as the psychologist would say, our habitual projections of that strife from the world around us, and realize that we should be so busy killing the selfishness within that we really have not the time, much less the will to blow up our neighbour. And when a few more individuals recognize that the war within implies a friendly tolerance of those about one, and of their ways of living and internal fighting, the Hitlers and Stalins and even the unpleasant fellow next door may provoke in everyman a smile, rather than an H-bomb, or even a bow and arrow.

Deck Chair, Brighton

Men call it rest, a slave awhile set free
At peace upon the verge of warring day,
Each fretful moment's importunity
Resisted and refused and laid away.

O nobler peace, entirely to withdraw
From sound and thought of action, from the will
That sightless drives the instruments of war!
Oh to remove the body and be still,
Bereft of thought and hope and things thought-made!
Thus mind, refreshed with light, returning slow,
Sees but illusion and sees, unafraid,
Earth, body, thought, as void, as formless flow;
Illusion all, as Mind, the fighter knows,
One only Mind, at war in full repose.

IO

The Conquest of Death

Nearly all in the West fear death, the death of the physical body. Against this inevitable event all manner of charms and gestures and evasive descriptions are employed; diseases which have a high death rate are taboo in polite conversation. All to do with the subject — funerals, mourning and the like — are matters of gloom and despondency, and cheerfulness in the presence of death is a lamentable breach of behaviour.

In the East it is otherwise, and Chinese coolies will cheerfully dice for the deceased's possessions, using the coffin as a table for their play. The Taoist philosopher, Chuang-Tzu, could explain at once his joyous frame of mind soon after his wife's decease. 'When she died,' he admitted, 'I could not help being affected by her death. Soon, however, I remembered that she had already existed in a previous state before birth, without form or substance; that while in that unconditioned condition, substance was added to spirit; that this substance then assumed form; and that the next stage was birth. And now, by virtue of a further change she is dead, passing from one stage to another like the sequence of spring, summer, autumn and winter.' To celebrate her temporary sleep with weeping and wailing seemed to Chuang-Tzu to proclaim himself ignorant of natural laws. His philosophy may not be accepted, but at least it was applied; in the West we glibly talk of 'life everlasting', but behave as though the loved one were being seen off to hell.

The difference of attitude is based on a profoundly different philosophy, which derives in turn from a greater knowledge of the complex nature of 'self'. In Western belief the life of a human being is bounded by the birth and dissolution of the physical body. To this must be added the doctrine, which is unproved, unreasonable, and contrary to the known facts of natural processes, that the soul, whatever that may be, duly 'saved' by the minimum of the individual's effort and the maximum of God's, continues to exist eternally in a state of unearned and unjustified perfection. Is it therefore surprising that thinking men increasingly reject both parts of this belief, refusing to accept that something created in time should last eternally or, conversely, that that which is to live eternally has not existed since the beginning of the convenient illusion men call time?

What is a reasonable explanation of the phenomenon of life and death, which is scientific in that it springs from observable premises, and passes via reasonable hypothesis to definite and fear-destroying ends? It is the Buddhist teaching of self, its nature, cause and ending.

The Buddhist explanation begins with the verifiable fact of change. All things are *anicca*, changing and impermanent, and the physical body, produced by its parents, is no exception to the rule. If there is one certainty in life it is the body's ultimate death, and only the intense dislike of this fact, born of the mind's illusion, blinds our eyes to the further fact that the unknown elements in the experience of death are three; that is to say, when and where and how, in this particular life period, it will occur.

What dies at death? The visible answer is the physical body, in the East called *rupa*. In a way this death is itself illusion, for putrefaction is a form of life, a process of change, and a putrefying body is as full of life as its recent possessor when consciously alive. It is not life which has left the body but the co-ordinating factor of consciousness which made that body a unit of life, as distinct from a million million units of life pursuing their several ends. In life there was a general to command the army; in death the component parts thereof proceed to fight for their several purposes.

The East, with its thousands of years of tested and verified research, describes at length the invisible and finer 'bodies' which also die at the body's death, and those which do not. Here we are not concerned with *jiva* or *prana*, the life-force of the body which flows through a golden web which, when it coils up from the feet and passes out through the top of the head, produces the actual moment of 'death'. Nor are we here concerned with the 'astral double', the true seat of the physical senses, of the emotions, and of most psychic phenomena; nor with the lower *siddhis* (Pali: *iddhis*) or powers beloved of the idly curious, but daily used in the East with all other faculties. All these are fully described in a score of text-books in English, and correlated with psychology in such works as *This World and That*, by Bendit and Payne. On the understanding of the nature of self the West is in its infancy; so far we have not advanced beyond the vague though useful 'body, soul and spirit' of St Paul. Yet in a civilization which believes that the most important factor in self is the physical body, and which regards the emotions and the mind as attributes still scarcely separated from the functions of the brain, it is enough if an enquiry into death is confined to that part of it which needs no theory, no debatable doctrine for its proof. The Theravada School of Buddhism describes in detail the five constituents of the personality of which the fifth is *rupa*, the physical body; it is enough to know that all alike are subject to the Signs of Being, and that even *Vijnana* (consciousness), which needs the body for its functioning, dies at the body's death.

Now the process of *anicca* (change), works through a cyclic law. All that is born must pass through the process of birth, growth, decay and death, though the cycle be so swift that the fastest camera cannot follow the process, or so large and slow that empires rise and fall while a range of mountains passes through its geological day. As the cycles are infinitely various in duration and size, a single unit of life, if the term be acceptable, is at any moment in a dozen places in as many cycles. The body, for example, moves to a zenith at the age of thirty-five, and thereafter passes to a slow decay. But the intellect of a man may reach its zenith at sixty or seventy, even as his artistic output as a poet may have flowered and died in his twenties. Sometimes cycles coincide, as in the 'change of life', which affects both body and mind, but the size and range of cycle is almost infinite, and, like the wheels in a watch, they are elaborately geared together.

If these are facts, and each may be verified from original experience, it is clearly wise to face them along with other natural phenomena, such as the weather, or the necessary functions of the body while still alive. It is well to meditate upon the fact of death as it affects oneself. That it will happen is certain; only the date is unknown. Do I fear to make a will, and if so, why? Can I visualize another in my job, in my home, enjoying my loved possessions? Parents, children, friends and relations will also sooner or later die, and a life based on the assumption that they, or any of them, will escape the law is foolishness. For the Buddhist doctrine is precise; there is no loss. Links of love and hate must have their recompense, for the law of karma knows no compromise. Love is a bond, for good or evil according to its purity, and those who love will walk together up the long road to perfection, life after life, until the last illusion — of separation—is overcome. Whatever it is that moves from life to life, a 'bundle of characteristics', 'a propelled continuum', a diminishing self or an expanding Self, these 'units of life' are equally bound by the law of karma, and love is indeed the fulfilling of the Law.

Yet men are fearful of death, and in their terror cry in the darkness for some assurance of immortality. The Egyptians went to enormous lengths to preserve the body as the home or 'base' of the ka, the astral double. In the same way men who should know better strive in the séance room to 'keep in touch' with 'the dear departed', not heeding, even denying the injury they do to the inner vehicles of the mediums. Nor do they seem to be aware of the evil which they cause to the ones they loved who, earthbound in the toils of this completely selfish longing, are held back from their normal progress on the inner planes until their karma calls them back for fresh experience.

The fear of death is one of the most powerful forces in man, for it is the fear of self-dissolution. This which we love so mightily, for which we strive so long, so blindly and so hard, the self, is loath to die. Philosophy will not persuade it to dissolve, nor the thought that Nirvana itself is a blowing out, as a candle is blown out, of the awareness of separation. The fear of death is the fear of the end of an illusion; so long as the illusion persists so long will the fear remain. Only the mind's expansion, beyond

the realm of emotion, beyond the illusion of the separate existence of this craving 'I', can let in the light of enlightenment by
which the pilgrim sees, beyond peradventure, that he and the
host of his brother pilgrims, the mountain, the Way and the end
of the Way, are one.

Death must be conquered, and conquered in life. Only then
will it have no terrors when, as the supreme experience of an
incarnation, only equalled by the hour of birth, it again appears.
The Japanese Samurai were perhaps the greatest warriors of all
time, for their training was mental as well as physical. Here was
no process of mass hypnotism, nor were they drugged with the
mantric effect of an emotional battle-cry. Singly, one by one,
they were trained in the mind's development to a point where
the love of self was vanquished. The desires of self for self were
slain in meditation, and the man who fought for his Lord fought
fearlessly as one who, having died already, does not fear to die.

There are ways of conquering death less strenuous, if less
complete, which all of us can master. First, we can meditate on
the facts, or, at least, the theory of rebirth. Whatever is born and
dies and comes to birth again is a growing something which was
not created by an omnipotent God at the baby's birth; nor does
it die when the body, as a garment laid aside, is sweetly burnt
and returned to its elements. In the long, long past and the painfully long future of the climb to Enlightenment there is scope
for the heart's assurance that death is indeed no ending. Yet how
much better it is to work for the death of the self, and so to die
now, and here, and deliberately, to the end that with the body's
death we do not die! If only we could drop this burden of self-
longing, or at least reduce the load, we should begin to die
gracefully and progressively, and in the process learn that to die
in this sense is to be free. For the body corruptible and mortal
moves on a spiral downward to an egocentric *dukkha* or
unhappiness. Only the man who gives up his life shall learn to
live, and if these are the platitudes of all great Teachers, they
are provably true for all who practise them.

Is the doctrine of rebirth, of a timeless, smooth continuum of
karma-bearing effort, difficult to understand? We work by day,
and when the evening comes lie down for a well-earned sleep. In
the morning we begin to work at the task of yesterday, but with

all of yesterday's experience, and wisdom and developed faculty. We do not fear to sleep. Why, then, do we fear to die? Perhaps the fear is of the thought of dying young, or even in middle age. But why should we die before the normal and 'allotted' span unless our own past action has decreed it so? There is no such thing as accident, and a man dies, as he was born, under the operation of unswerving law. If 'accident' deprives us of a limb, or of life itself, or of a friend's dear company, what was the cause of which this was the unloved effect? We may not know, but we do know that a cause, a thousandfold and complex cause, exists. Is it not wiser to pay the debt, and to be grateful that the unpleasant moment, like a dentist's interview, is over? Karma unfulfilled is a barrier on the path of progress; as we receive, accept and digest it, there is that much less between us and the goal, and the light which our self-begotten action barred us from perceiving pours into the mind.

We plan for tomorrow, and for months and years ahead. If we truly accept the doctrine of rebirth why do we not plan for the next life and the lives thereafter? For a man believes a doctrine when he behaves as if it were true. The nature of that which is reborn is quite immaterial. Whatever it is which moves from life to life it is 'self'-begotten, and that which sowed the seed must reap the harvest. Instead of the pause in middle age, when a man begins to look backward and to slow down his advance; instead of the halt in old age when the mind is turned into the past, the Buddhist lifts his eyes to the day's work when the night of rest is over. On that day we shall reap the effects of present causes. If the cause was good shall we fear the effect; if bad, is it not better to pay the debt, and speedily?

Here, then, is a picture of life and death wherein there is no fear of the unknown; only acceptance and a welcome for the known. The periods of life and death are as beads on a necklace, black and white alternately, that span the process of our slow becoming. The Buddhist can with confidence declare 'There is no death'. Death for him is the shadow on the face of life, for the opposite of death is birth, not life; that which is born must die. Life has no opposite, for life goes on; only its forms must change unceasingly. It is life which creates, uses and then destroys each form of life, whether yours or mine or that of the mountain, the empire or the fly. When the form can no longer express the life which is using it, it is broken by the force of life and 'dies'. When the light wears out its lamp the lamp is thrown away and a new one is provided. So, when life wears out the body, it should be cleanly and with little grief destroyed. Meanwhile, the life that uses forms and is yet confined in none of them moves on to its own high purposes.

Yet for each of us the night must fall, and the self, the blind and foolish self which still believes that it alone is real, resents the coming. *Sabbe dhamma anatta*—all things are without an immortal Self which separates them from the stream of life's becoming. Sooner or later, here or there, the man we knew, that muddled, changeable collection of a thousand attributes, will be dissolved. At the right time, in some other place and name and form, in new conditions which will be heir to old endeavour, the pilgrim treads again the mountain path to his own and the world's Enlightenment. Is this a matter for regret, or fear? He who believes it utterly has no fear; for him the fear of death and therefore death itself is ended. To the last breath of this life his face is set towards the stars of his unattainment, and his mind, in the eternal moment of his passing, fills with awareness of the union of life with THAT from which it came. Thereafter silence, rest, the digestion of a life's experience and then, rebirth as karma claims him.

Once more the pilgrim takes his staff in hand. The road lies clear before him, for the Guide has given him full details of this Way. All that he needs is to arise and once again 'walk on'. At the journey's end all life will welcome him.

When I am Dead

When I am dead, who dies, who dies,
    And where am I?
A dewdrop in a shining sea,
    An inmate in the sky?
Or do I rest awhile and thence
Return for new experience?

There's nothing changeless, heaven or hell
    Nor life's oblivion;
Only a heart at rest and then
    A further walking on.
We live and as we live we learn;
We die, and then again return.

Yet who returns, what comes again
    To fretful earth?
I know not. Only this I know;
There is a road that comes to birth
In everyman, and at the end
Shall brother know all life his friend.

II

Dharma. How It Works

Nearly all men have some 'God' who gives meaning and purpose to life. Such a concept may be inherited from family upbringing, formulated by personal study or be a subconscious remnant from some preceding life. Only Masters, Rishis, Roshis, call them by what name we will, having no sense of 'other', find no need for the God-concept in any form. You and I are still encumbered with some 'Father-image' which we project into the sky and worship; or an equally projected Teacher, alive or dead; or his writings which we regard as authority for Truth; or we may have a vague sense of what Edwin Arnold called 'the Power divine which moves to good'. Or we may, unaware of the fact, lean heavily on the idea of 'the Buddha within'. One day all of these must die.

Said the Bishop of Woolwich, 'Kill God, and find him alive'. Said a Zen master, 'If you meet the Buddha, kill him'. From concept, then, however lofty, we must move to that which lies 'beyond', the Namelessness, Eckhart's 'Godhead' beyond God, Para-Brahman, what the Buddha called the 'Unborn, Un-originated, Unformed'; but we cannot lean on these.

I too lean, for a while at least, and my God is made of paper, any bit of paper, on which I have made a list of 'things to be done' which, when men meet together for a collective purpose, is called the Agenda.

The name of my God is Dharma. What does the word mean? Its basic meaning is to sustain. Other English terms are Law, Norm, Duty, Teaching. In the East Buddhism is called the

Buddha-dharma, or dhamma in the Pali form. For me my God provides a platform which sustains me; he gives meaning to life, and the purpose and agenda for this life; also the means to cope with this agenda, and the power to achieve it. As such he is surely a hard-working God, and I am at present satisfied. He is to me Law; in the sense that when I oppose my personal will against God's will, that of the universe, I suffer. I therefore believe in Tennyson's ideal,

> to live by law,
> Acting the law we live by without fear;
> And because right is right to follow right
> Were wisdom in the scorn of consequence.

The range of dharma is complete. It includes the whole day's work—and rest. But the difficulties awaiting the devotee of this my God are enormous. First, to know what is *my* dharma in any particular set of circumstances. Then to accept its limitations, the blinkers which prevent me following after false gods for foolish purposes. Where does the unconscious fit in with my conscious understanding of God's purpose? I must allow for types, my complex own included. I must allow for dharma transcendent and immanent, see the Unborn in the born, the ultimate Life-principle using the best of me, which strives to control the worst of me, to assist the high purpose of the whole of me, the ultimate, inseverable Whole.

What, then, is *my* dharma? Enter the word duty. Why do we so hate that term? Is it because it represents what we know we ought to do as distinct from what we *want* to do? But I have used the word ought, which connotes a debt we owe. Dharma, duty, and debt. Our dharma is a list of the debts we owe—to society, humanity, Life, the ultimate Whole. So we had better pay them as and when they are presented and fall due. As such, dharma is its own authority; it needs no Law-giver. It is in itself intelligent, living Law.

What is owed? The answer lies in Karma, and the time for payment is provided by Rebirth. The living and intelligent law of karma is based on harmony, the unbreakable harmony of the manifest universe as an expression of the Unborn. Man breaks it and pays for the breakage. He calls this suffering and complains of it, but *he* pushed the pendulum. If it swings back and knocks him painfully shall he complain? What breaks the harmony? I, while under the domination of the illusion of 'me'. The ego wants, for itself, and helps itself. The Law adjusts (a frightening term) the damage to the offender, and he pays, some time, somewhere, to the full; none shall stay the cold hand of that retribution. Thus we learn, if we are wise, to 'go and sin no more'.

The difficulties are indeed immense. How *does* one find one's dharma? Must I accept the limitations involved? And what of the unconscious, in the Western meaning of the term? Will it adopt my own adoption of this immanent-transcendent God? His limitations must be faced and borne, for we are all of different types in our human make-up. To the introvert and extravert types of Jungian psychology we must add the older classifications of the East, the Jnana Yogin who is at best the Sage; the Bhakti Yogin who follows the way of devotion, to the Ideal and its earthly representatives; and the Karma Yogin, the man of action, of Right Action at his best, for whom the perpetual service of all forms of life is a sufficient ideal. But in all there is the self which must be allowed to die; the Self or reincarnating 'bundle of characteristics' or character, which should, but seldom does, control the ego-will of self or 'me', and the 'Unborn, Unoriginated'—the Beyond of any Self, of which the man we know *should* be the conscious conduit pipe.

But the first is the hardest question—What is my dharma in any place and time? The answer lies in the word duty. I ask again, why do we hate it so? Because when young we learnt to equate it with something we did not wish to do, which conflicted with pleasure, and the desires of 'I'? Surely it is a debt owed by the part to the Whole, imposed, not by an outside Power or cosmic God but by our own past action. Let us feel for it, listen for it, find it in any situation, and pay. It is its own authority for payment.

Thus dharma and karma are closely interlinked. My dharma now is an invoice of past debts presented for payment. I must accept, fully and without equivocation or attempt to escape, the debts to be paid. 'Projections'—attempts to blame all and sundry for my own past folly—will be found of no avail, and we must learn to withdraw them. None other is to blame for our body, home or circumstance, our friends and enemies, our job and place in the world. We made it all; let us accept and use and better it. We shall try to run away; into pleasure, and religion, ill-health—even into a Vihara, but the *Dhammapada* is right. 'Not in the sky, nor in the sea, nor in a cave in the mountains can a man escape from his evil deeds.' Some karma is like Destiny; it is too late to avoid it. Much may be modified by subsequent wise action, or even by its mere acceptance. As I accept the karma coming to me it becomes my dharma, the next thing to be done, and a list of such things, on a daily piece of paper, is indeed the outer form and semblance of my 'God'.

But all, each trivial thing to be done, must be done 'rightly' for this is the meaning of *Samma* in the Buddha's Noble Eightfold Path. We need *Right* views, *Right* action, *Right* mind-development in all its forms. In Western terms this surely implies right motive, means and time and place. The motive is of supreme importance. *Why* do we tread the Path, or try to? Why do we seek Enlightenment, and for whom? If for self we are but enlarging the ego which it is the purpose of all Buddhist practice to destroy. Note the order of events imposed in *The Voice of the Silence*. 'The first step is to live to benefit mankind. To practise the six glorious virtues is the second.' The means are infinite in number and form, and that which is right on one occasion for one person at that time may be wrong in other circumstances for a different person at some other time. And timing is itself important. As the Arabs say, 'You cannot mount the camel that has not yet come nor the camel that has gone'. Let each thing be done, then, as soon as it appears—why later? Let it be done because it is to be done, for no other reason is required. Let it be done with full concentration as best we know how, and then dropped, and forgotten. There will be the next thing waiting to be done. If this sounds feverish action without pause it should not be so. The next thing to be done may be to rest, fully and completely, whether for an hour, the night, or between two lives.

There are things to be done and not to be done, and the choice at times is extremely difficult. We must help when opportunity arises, at whatever cost to self. 'There is no such thing as sacrifice', as the Lama said in Talbot Mundy's *OM*, 'there is only opportunity to serve.' But 'there is danger in another's duty', as the Bhagavad Gita warns, and it is not easy for the average Westerner to learn to mind his own business. Yet we must remember, 'Inaction in a deed of mercy becomes an action in a deadly sin'.

Why all this 'doing', it is sometimes asked? Can we not just 'be'? But how do we attain to right being, save by long lives of right doing? And are not the two in the end the same? Prajna (Wisdom) and Karuna (Compassion) are, says the Mahayana teaching, one and inseverable. By Wisdom we see what is to be done, and it is not true compassion which has no eyes. By Compassion we make our Wisdom wise; for until applied it is not Wisdom. In a word, we only *know* what we have *done*, and such is the Wisdom, as I understand it, of all the schools of Buddhism.

We find our own way to right action, and tread it as we go. He who tells his neighbour what he, the neighbour, should do in given circumstances is a fool. He does not and he cannot know. 'If I were you' is a silly beginning to any remark. You are not, and you never will be anyone else. Mind your own business; it is, or should be, a full-time task for twenty-four hours a day.

But in the ideal, I, even as Self at its human best, am not the actor in any act. I am a conduit pipe for the universal will of the 'Unborn, Unoriginated, Unformed', of which the Universe and all we know is but a periodic coming forth in manifestation. As the Patriarch Hui Neng explained, 'We are already enlightened. What differs between us is that some know it and some do not.' Let us get out of the way of the Buddha within and let him get on with his own high purposes!

What calls to action? The head says, 'I see a job to be done', and looks no further. The heart says, 'I feel the suffering of a fellow being. Let me help.' If this be so, and this is duty, how is duty 'cold', or the very thought of it unwelcome? Rather it is a perpetual joy and satisfaction, come wet or fine, or well or ill, at any time and place on any occasion.

What are the needs of dharma, the demands of my God? Perpetual concentration on the job in hand, akin to the Theravada discipline of 'right-mindfulness'. Then 'guts'—I know no prettier term for what I mean, the developed will to dominate the demands of self when they interfere, to walk on and walk on though the Way be dark or difficult or dull. And some vision of the end to be achieved and the means for doing it. These come, as all else, by perpetual experience. If the task be deemed too difficult, remember a great explorer's words. 'The difficult takes time; the impossible takes a little longer.' Or the advice of the Master K.H. to his correspondent, A. P. Sinnett, 'We have one word for all aspirants, Try'.

Thus dharma is my companion and my guide, and the means which is itself the end. He is like the carrot on the donkey's nose, the ever receding ideal, the light on the summit of Everest, the welcome on the doorstep of 'my Father's home'. Meanwhile one's dharma is ever the world's need. We must help, 'until the last blade of grass has entered Buddahood'.

But there is even more to it than this. We must teach; 'there will be some whose eyes are scarce covered with the dust of illusion'. There is always someone needing the wisdom we have already gained. It is our dharma, as it will be his karma, to give it him.

And the goal of it all? It lies in our choosing, to accept the reward of duty done—and it is a high reward—or be so utterly dedicated to the common weal that such a guerdon lacks attraction. For these few—and they will ever be the few—the goal is to be so one with dharma that the self is gone. For these there will be meaning in the words of *The Voice of the Silence*— 'Remain unselfish to the endless end'.

12

Karma and Rebirth

Karma is the living law, perhaps the supreme law of the universe, which the seekers of Enlightenment must use in the development of the total self towards its spiritual fulfilment. It operates on all planes, at all times, to all things and in all circumstances. He who studies the law and learns to use it wisely is only expanding the process of science which discovers and learns to apply the laws of the physical plane, such as gravity. But in truth it is science, with its awareness that action and reaction are equal and opposite, which is using a limited aspect of the total law which, as karma, was known to man at the dawn of history.

The Sanskrit word *karma* (Pali : *kamma*) has three meanings : the basic meaning is action, thence action-reaction as an inseverable unit, and the law which governs their relation, and thirdly, the results of action, in the sense of the net resultant of a long series of acts by an individual or group. It is in this sense that Buddhists loosely speak of a man's 'good karma', or point to the 'evil karma' now being suffered by a group or nation for its collective action in days gone by.

As such the law is profound and immensely difficult, and if we understand it to the full we should be masters of the universe. For the cosmos cannot be partly ruled by law and partly the child of chaos. Either cause and effect hold sway or they do not; there can be no exceptions, although the complexity of the inter-relationship may be utterly beyond our present intellect to grasp. This law is indeed the key to all events in the world of time and space, and it is worth the courage needed to face what a full acceptance of it implies. For if karma is true it follows that luck, chance, coincidence and fate are words to be no more used. No man has luck, whether good or bad, and nothing occurs by chance. Coincidence is the 'falling together' of events by cause-effect, however obscure that sequence, and fate is a term for banked-up causes so near their discharge that no further cause can ward off the imminent effect.

Such thoughts, applied to the daily round, are at first profoundly disturbing. I may meet a long-lost friend who is newly arrived from Australia. We meet in a street which I have not entered before, nor he. We greet one another, exchange a few words and part. Was this coincidence? The mathematical odds against it extend to a dozen noughts. Was it mere coincidence? If not, have the powers of heaven and earth for a thousand years conspired to bring us face to face that morning at that place to say 'Hullo'?

And what is luck, but a label attached to the consequences of my own past action? And what is fate but those effects which now *must* happen? These thoughts must 'give us pause', but which is the nobler attitude of mind, to 'hope' that all will be well, yet to rail at destiny when things go wrong; or to accept the truth that all is happening because it must, that all that happens happens 'right', and all things do in fact work well? If the latter be true then cause alone is of prime importance, and the emphasis of thought is changed from the sufferance of effects to the importance of a nobler causing. Henceforth the mind will live increasingly on the plane of causes and learn to suffer, that is, to endure effects.

What is this law which so much of the world obeys and has used so widely for so long? Is it purely mechanical and blind? Or is it alive, as all the processes of thought, emotion, and our bodies are inter-related and alive? The Buddhist answer is clear, that there is nothing dead, that all the universe is but the outward seeming of Mind-only, and that every part of this 'becoming', by whatever name described, is one; one life, one living law and one Enlightenment.

This correlation of an infinite number of causes makes for an immense complexity of effects. But if life is indeed one, and time is a convenient illusion, it follows that the correlation of cause-effect is wider than mere sequence of events. Yet we see the relationship most clearly as a line of sequence, and so long as our lives are consciously moulded in the light of the one life, it matters not that we, the infinitesimal knots in the web, can only handle cause-effect, and further cause-effect, in moulding all things and ourselves just so much 'nearer to the heart's desire'. It is easy to see karma as the law of equilibrium, and its working as the adjustment of a balance disturbed. If a pendulum is pressed away it will return with the force which pushed it, and to the place whence it was pushed away. He that disturbed the pendulum must suffer the effect until the force is neutralized in the acceptance, and harmony restored.

Between man and man the law works out as love. 'Compassion is no attribute. It is the law of laws, eternal harmony, the fitness of all things, the law of Love eternal.' And the precision with which the balance is restored is frightening to him who leaves his debts unpaid. 'Not in the sky, nor in the sea, nor in a cave in the mountains can a man escape from his evil deeds.' And he is a fool to try.

The perfect act has no result. Where there is no 'self' to push the pendulum there is no self to receive the return, and cause-effect is ended for that doer. When every act has become dispassionate, impersonal, and done because it is 'right', there is no motive in the act, good or ill, and the ultimate aim of 'purposelessness' is attained. Nor is this an impossible ideal. To use a homely analogy, when a man in front of you drops a glove and you pick it up and return it, did you act from a thought-out motive? Or in fact did neither thought nor emotion enter your mind as you did what was obviously right, spontaneously? Yet if all living things so helped one another, without thought of self or hope of reward, in crises great and small, how large the difference to human life, how small the swing of the pendulum!

The law, then, can be used and freely used, and it cannot be 'interfered with'. All that we do is the result of our own past causes, for we are in fact the net resultant of our own past thought and action. It follows that all that we do, and all that is done to us, happens because it must so happen. The Good

Samaritan of the Christian New Testament was not 'interfering' with the karma of him he helped, while he that passed by suffered the grave loss of an opportunity. It is your karma that you should be helped, as you are, or left unaided as you may be, and it is your friend's good karma to have you as his friend. Away, then, with all thoughts of interference. Is the law of gravity disturbed when you hold an umbrella over your lady friend? Yet you have interfered, it would seem, with the sequence of drops of water and the spoiling of her new hat.

The avalanche which sweeps down the mountain cannot be stayed. Such karma is 'ripe' for reception, and no new cause of our devising can stay the conclusion of cause-effect. Such karma has the force of destiny, or fate. All else is changeable. There is an old, oft-quoted prayer : 'Grant us the courage to change those things which should be changed; grant us the patience to accept those things which cannot be changed. And above all grant us the wisdom to know the difference!'

Most situations may be altered by the addition of some new cause, just as the movement of an object pushed by a dozen men may be altered in speed or direction by the strength of another man. But even when a situation is too powerful to be changed one's personal reaction to it is at all times changeable. It may be that I cannot stop it raining but I can control, or should be able to control, my physical, emotional and mental reaction to the fact of rain.

Fate, then, in the sense of a force which we cannot affect and can only accept with patience and humility, is a doctrine only true for such karma as is over-ripe to change. Towards such fate we can but develop the courage to bear such ills as we have created for ourselves by previous action. Free will and pre-destination, the delight of the school debating society, are not one of the 'pairs of opposites' but the same truth from opposing points of view. Our lives are to a large extent predestined by our own past actions, but the force which created these conditions is as free as ever to remould them or to modify them either at the causal or the receiving end.

But if all in the universe is karma-made, then so am I. It follows that I must accept myself for what I am before I can deliberately change it. Having made myself and all of myself it is useless to complain of the body I had from my parents, or of the sex or class or race to which that body belongs. Still less have I any right to complain to an outside cause for any lack of bodily beauty or health or skill; rather should I be ashamed of my own past folly that made me so. If the garment of the mind, the personality, be self-created, so in a different way are the circumstances about it. True, it was not in this life that I made my body's environment, but it is by law that I am where I am. I chose, in the sense of creating magnetic links towards the whole of my environment, and all about me, body, parents, temperament and job are self-created and must be, if at all, self-changed.

The method of change is twofold, either by altering circumstances or by changing my reaction, physical and mental, towards it. The first is extrovert activity, and all men see it; the second lies in the mind. Thus the alleged antithesis of heredity versus environment is, like predestination and free will, falsely imagined. I 'made', in the sense that I brought myself into, my parents' body; I made in the same way my initial environment. Thereafter I begin to change my body and all about me, and I change, by all I think and do, my reaction to that changing circumstance. I can, if I think it helpful, and most men do, complain of my heredity and present environment. It is pleasant to say, and believe, that 'if only' things were otherwise I could do such different things and be so different. But it is quite untrue. For those differences would only exist if I made them so, and if I made them so I should be different too.

Complain then, if you will, of all about you, of the Government, of your employers, of your ailments, and your landlord, of your family, your lack of capital and your job. But as you chose or made them so it would surely be more dignified to change them, if you will and can, and meanwhile to blame yourself for your creation. This is the practical doctrine of acceptance, to take things as they are because you made them so, and to blame yourself, without self-pity or untrue remorse, for everything about you of which you do not approve. Thus karma is indeed the law of laws, and knows no compromise. Its work is to adjust effect to cause on every plane, whatever the size of the causing unit of life, whether man or group or nation. It does not reward or punish; it adjusts. We are punished by our sins, not for them. He who works with nature flows on the river of life to the everlasting sea; he who resists is broken miserably.

But like all other laws of nature, karma may be used. How? A man may take stock of himself as he would of his own business. What are his assets, and his liabilities? What is his output, and how could it be more? What stands in the way of his further expansion? What new powers are needed to that end?

Having taken stock let him reorganize this highly personal concern. Much must be scrapped of habit and outmoded prejudice; much must be slowly replaced and new attainment acquired. A new spirit is needed, perhaps in the Chairman of the Board; stock that is seen to be worthless, of old beliefs and values, had best be destroyed.

But when the new broom is applied in action the office staff may prove to be difficult. Habits of mind, emotion and body have had their way too long to be lightly given notice; they may, indeed, make strenuous attempts to sack the proprietor. Creditors will press for payment; debtors seem unduly slow to pay. If Rome was not built in a day a totally new man, converted to a Way of which the end is self-Enlightenment, will not be built by a mere resolution. But once the resolve is made there are but two rules to the opening of that Way; begin and walk on!

The doctrine of rebirth is a necessary corollary to that of karma. If a man is responsible for the consequences of his thoughts and acts, he cannot escape the appropriate results by the death of his physical body. Even the suicide returns again and again to the situation he refused to face until he has accepted, in every sense of the term, the products of his own imagining.

Of the nature of that which is reborn, of the prevalence of the doctrine and the problems which it solves, and of the avenues of thought flung open by this vast extension of the 'allotted span', little need here be said. Books have been written on the subject, and all may study them. But Buddhism, which stresses the futility of speculation, and trains the student's mind to the immediate task in hand, finds little profit in discussing matters which do not lead to the heart's enlightenment. Whether the bundle of attributes which is reborn be called a self, or soul, or character, it is like all else in the universe for ever changing, growing, and becoming something more. It is not an 'immortal soul' which, possessed by you, is different from that possessed by me. It is in fact the product of that which dies, and whatever the form may be, we are here and now, with every breath we draw, creating it.

The value of the Buddhist doctrine of rebirth is that it shatters the end-wall of our present life. Instead of a final judgment leading to heaven or hell, or a period of purgatory followed by eternal bliss, which equally offend the sense of justice and the heart's belief, the Buddhist offers a vista of an ever-rising path which climbs the mountain to a range of view now past imagining.

How long the path may be depends for any man on where he stands today and his speed of travel. These are his past and present choosing, but the beginning of the Way is here and now, and karma and rebirth are the means of treading it.

Youth in Age

The twilight falls. Inevitable hands
Draw the soft curtains of the fading day.
All changes, grows, grows old. Nature demands
A cycle absolute of growth-decay.
Birth follows, of the flesh, and every hour
The wakening mind, when limbs of courage leap
To fresh awareness widens, bursts in flower
Awhile in splendour, till the body's sleep.

So life, resistless, strides upon the hills
Of our becoming and with laughing tread
Creates and uses and in using kills,
Till every form with force of life lies dead.

The dissolution of recurring night
Awaits the body. For the spirit, light.

13

The Buddhist Middle Way

In his First Sermon the Buddha spoke of two extremes to be avoided, that of devotion to the pleasures of sense and that of self-mortification, both of which he described as 'unworthy and unprofitable'. Avoiding them, he said, he had gained knowledge of a Middle Path which led to enlightenment and he described the eight steps on the Way.

This concept of a Middle Way gives rise to far more subtle problems than the avoidance of these two extremes, for it opens for examination and right reaction the whole field of duality. In Buddhist metaphysics the Absolute, whether viewed as the Dharmakaya, the Alayavijnana, Sunyata or the 'Unborn, Unoriginated, Unformed' is manifested, enters existence, becomes relative, in a field of duality. In the simplest of all formulae, that of the *Tao Te Ching*, 'Tao begets One; One begets two; Two begets three; Three begets all things'. Or again, 'From Eternal Non-existence, the antecedent of heaven and earth, we serenely observe the mysterious beginning of the universe. From eternal existence we clearly see the apparent distinctions. These two are the same in source and become different when manifested.' The Buddha advised against all speculation on ultimates, but the above seems to be good Buddhism.

In any event the Opposites are with us; we live in a bi-polar field. We observe in ourselves the differences of sex, of psychological temperament. We notice in-breathing and out-breathing, night and day. In nature we observe the play of positive-negative, growth and decay, not merely temporal but as forces operating to produce unceasing tension, as two protagonists in a constant war which none can ever win. And the relationship is not static. 'Man walks upon two legs' as I once observed, and all progression is from side to side. Exaggerate the movement and we change the simile to the pendulum which swings, in a wide or modest movement, to and fro. But the pendulum makes visible the fact that two involves relationship, the third ingredient which in living tension is the trinity of spiritual becoming. From the point from which the pendulum is hung is a 'higher third' from which to view the complementary opposites and the way to use them, and finally transcend their seeming difference.

How, then, do we react to the observed and admitted opposites, to the 'other view' which for the moment is not our own? There seem to be four ways; to choose one or the other, to compromise between them, to lift to the standpoint of a 'higher third' or to achieve the Zen goal of Non-duality. The first two move in duality; the third, though still bound in the fetters of concept, is at least a vision of the true relationship. Only the fourth, achieved in 'moments of no-time', is free of the pendulum, the see-saw, and the tension of these ultimately non-existent forces in nature and the mind.

We should, however, first examine the spectacles through which perforce we regard the opposites, and in particular that which is further from our own proclivity. We do not now stand in the middle; in every aspect of our life we have, deliberately or by the 'conditioning' of birth, education or environment, allowed ourselves to stand on one bank of the river of life, with some intolerance of those who were foolish enough to choose or be led to stand on the other. Thus we are male or female, old or young, of the East or West. By temperament we are introvert or extravert, leaders or followers, all for action or striving rather to be. It surely follows that we should be more tolerant of the other fellow, equally right/wrong, and be less swift to judge him with our ignorant, lop-sided view and definite disapproval. In any event, do we have to express an opinion, presume to judge?

And so to the four ways of regarding the opposites. We can choose, as at times we must, though our choice is more limited by our karma than we lightly suppose. And in some cases such a definite choice may be laudable. Between honesty and dishonesty, loyalty and disloyalty, we firmly choose and without apology, but the definition of such terms, and their meaning in a particular situation, is man-made and variable, and even for 'good' and 'evil' there is, as we shall see, a 'higher third'. More often we compromise, for it is rooted in the mind to strive for the middle way. After all, the dharma is rightly translated, among a dozen terms, as the Norm. We love the normal man; we suspect and slightly fear the extremist, the man so different from ourselves. Yet compromise should always move from strength, from deliberate selection of the right point of view and action. In brief, stand where you will but don't wobble!

Now let us look more closely at some of the pairs of opposites. At least we should know, and clearly, whether we are more drawn to the Arhat or the Bodhisattva ideal. These are surely complementary, but there are Buddhists who will not have it so. For some the Arhat ideal of the Theravada School is right, and that is that; yet for the Mahayanist, self-salvation is less important than integration with all beings. Compassion is looking outwards to the limits of manifestation rather than upwards to the final goal for this particular aspect of All-Mind; for those who have taken the Bodhisattva Vow to postpone salvation 'till the last blade of grass shall enter into Enlightenment' the need of all the world is paramount. Yet it seems that many of the Zen School take the view—and who shall call them 'wrong'?—that a break-through to the plane of Non-duality is the first and vital requirement; compassion, assistance to all beings, follows. To which his neighbour may reply, in the words of *The Voice of Silence*, 'The first step is to live to benefit mankind'.

Of the same type of antithesis is Prajna/Karuna, Wisdom/Compassion, which may be paraphrased as to be or to do, to aim at wisdom, and then to work it out in compassion for all, or to work for all in loving service and thereby to attain the wisdom needful for its full accomplishment. It matters not; each of us is child of his previous karma, each must in the end not only see that the other is equally right, as the two sides of a coin, but acquire the grace to allow his brother to get on with his own pre-chosen way; and this allowance must not be unwilling, negative tolerance but a willingness to help one's neighbour to work out his own salvation, in his own way, with diligence.

Now only does a firm Middle Way begin, with a lift in thought, and thence in actual consciousness, to the Higher Third. The swing of the pendulum is now reduced; we are walking straighter with less deviation from side to side. We see, at least with intellect, that beyond both true and false is Truth; that there is Beauty beyond our present views on the beautiful and ugly; that pleasure-pain can alike be now transcended, and that some day we shall truly *see* that 'Form is Emptiness and the very Emptiness is Form'. Action is more impersonal; motive moves from that which pays to that which is felt to be right in the special circumstances. While accepting the tramlines of 'ripe' karma, which cannot be avoided, we are more careful not to create fresh karma by thoughtless action or inaction for which we shall have to pay. The choice grows narrower, more subtle. There will be conflict of duties. We must remember that 'there is danger in another's duty' but not forget that 'inaction in a deed of mercy becomes an action in a deadly sin'. We shall be learning to drop the foolish word 'authority'. None exists; not even the words of the Buddha himself, as no less an 'authority' than the Buddha himself in his famous Kalama Sutta insists. Instead, we shall be toying with that lovely phrase—the ultimate advice in mind-control—to 'let the mind abide nowhere'. By-passing all scriptures and all that any teacher has to say, we shall, while respecting every finger that points to the moon, be mindful only of the moon. This habit will make it easier to understand the truth that *every* statement is wrong, whenever made by any man, for it was made in duality and is therefore one-sided, incomplete, and in the final synthesis its opposite is just as true!

For we are now at the entrance of the Middle Way which has no middle. Just as the Theravada doctrine of *anatta*—no permanent 'self' in any thing—was raised by the great minds of the Mahayana to *Sunyata,* the emptiness so empty that it is even empty of emptiness, so the temperate path which avoids the extremes of self-indulgence and asceticism is raised by the Zen School to its ultimate meaning—and beyond. While the meditating Buddhist whose aim is samadhi, the calm sea of the thought-less mind, is left to his meditation, the man of Zen goes marching on, singing his foolish songs and talking inspired and witless nonsense which, dismissed as such by his intellectual fellows, is indeed non-sense, being beyond, most joyously beyond, the limitations of the thinking mind.

For such a man the Middle Way can have no middle, for all in manifestation, every thing that is, is on one side or the other of it. Along the razor's edge which has no width nor destination the man of Zen, unbound by choice, his own or others', serene in the Oneness that knows not self or other, moves happily, for 'what could go wrong?'

As to choosing, he finds Hui Neng was right, that 'All distinctions are falsely imagined'. As to action, he sees that *wei wu wei*, to act without acting, is alone right action. As to motive, when subject and object are alike seen as illusion the only purpose must be purposeless—'There, it's done!'

These are words, but the man who for a day, an hour or a moment moves on such a way will recognize their meaning. For us the use of simile may help. We read of 'the still centre of the turning world', of the need to find and hold our centre of gravity. We admire the rock unmoved in the centre of a raging sea. Again, we read of a circle whose centre is everywhere and circumference nowhere. But this implies that the rock in the raging sea has no location, that it moves as occasion demands even as a fencer's centre of gravity, as he moves at speed, is ever between his feet.

At the middle of the Middle Way there is, first, an awareness of an immovable centre, unshaken by tempest without or doubt within. Then the sense of location disappears. The immovable centre is everywhere, in any situation. Having no place we cannot be moved from it; we can be, and willingly let ourselves be, pushed about. Motion, indeed, is found to be commensurate with life. The still centre moves as we move, floating upon the placeless, timeless Essence of Mind. But when there is neither here nor there, whither we move is of little consequence. The Middle Way not only has no middle but, as a way, no direction. Asked 'What is Tao?', a master replied, 'Walk on!'

But as we move we do not move off centre. Solidly based on the centre within, which is the centre of the universe, we are unbound in place and time. As the Chinese say, 'the place that is nowhere, that is the true home'. On such a journey distinctions evaporate, and our study of positive-negative, subject-object and even nirvana-samsara is more and more illumined by the light within.

The points of the oxy-acetylene flame move nearer, and sparks begin to leap the space between. We suddenly know that *of course* 'all form is emptiness and the very emptiness is form'. How silly we were to doubt it! The tramlines of old thought and choice are now dissolving; the river banks are no more opposite; the flow of stillness is a sense of stillness as we flow.

And the Middle Way? We look to see where the mind is caught up to the right or left, for every choice is now seen as an attachment which prevents the mind from 'alighting nowhere'. Thoughts are so many hooks which bind us to the illusion of circumstance. Yet, as Hui Neng enjoined, 'We must stand aloof from circumstances, and on no account allow them to influence our mind'.

And the ultimate middle? The non-existent, utterly void middle which thought can never find? Most of us just wonder what the view must be from such an eminence. Or is it an eminence? Is it just the view out of the window—the lamp-post, the street and the passers-by, but no longer seeing them as different, as opposite, at war? If that is all let us open our eyes and newly see; and then walk on.

14

Meditation: Its Place in Western Buddhism

In due course there will be a Western Buddhism, even as there is now the Buddhism of Ceylon, or Tibetan Buddhism. The West will absorb and use what it needs of all existing Buddhist schools, and slowly devise its own. It has begun to do so. At the same time there will co-exist a few of the present schools as such; in particular, Theravada and the Zen school, both of which satisfy a spiritual need of the Western mind. These, however, will be modified, and are already being modified by Western usage.

What will be the place of meditation in this field? Clearly there must be, as described in the Noble Eightfold Path which is the heart of Buddhism, a stage of deliberate mind-control and development, to follow 'right' views and Sila, the moral life. Note the order. In the Pali canon, doctrine and right living take precedence of the meditation systems of the later Abhidhamma which, though stressed in Burma are little used in Ceylon. In the Zen School of Japan, meditation, in the sense of long periods of 'sitting' is paramount; in Tibet it plays a very important part. What will be its place in Western Buddhism? It is pure conceit to believe that a few well-chosen leaders will decide. Whatever these few proclaim and preach the Western Buddhist mind will produce its own 'Buddhism', and is at present building it. Already we know—from the sale of literature—that it is not (at present) interested in Buddhist metaphysics or in Buddhist art, nor in ritual, nor in what it knows of Soto Zen. It likes the principles and practice of the Theravada, which is surely 'Basic Buddhism', and it welcomes the Mahayana emphasis on compassion. It flirts with the mysticism of the later school, and shows surprising aptitude for Zen. The few of us monastically bent by temperament are happy to meditate all day; a large number of us are quite unimpressed by the need for it. Is it wise, therefore, to take the Western would-be Buddhist on the doorstep and sit him down to meditate? Not long ago I watched a provincial Buddhist group, already well established in the study of first principles, just fade away when a bhikkhu assumed control and made them meditate instead. Long periods of sitting may be right for Zen in Japan and for neophytes in Burma and Tibet, but the Western mind is differently framed. Of course the thinking mind must sooner or later be controlled, developed, and supplied with the force of will for a break-through to non-thinking, a direct awareness of Non-duality. But at what stage?

The Western mind is steeped in its own traditions of thought and feeling, with Christianity as its built-in religion, and a fascinating blend of strictly rational and 'scientific' thinking and an irrational, poetic love of the Beyond, which erupts in a wide variety of forms, from Welsh mysticism to Alice in Wonderland. Will such a mind, young as world-thought goes, virile and magnificent with self-assurance, happily take to sitting still and, in a phrase already charged with contempt, contemplating its navel?

What happens when the attempt is made? The superstructure of mental practice is built on the ruins of previous thought and feeling. This erstwhile palace of Christian theology and moral values, with a vast assembly of myth and symbol and irrational belief in the basement or subconscious mind, is left untouched by the would-be meditator. He builds on top of it. The new plant thrives on the watering can of fresh excitement. It seldom puts down roots. Is it surprising, then, that many of those who meditate—some say, most—'have a go' for quite long periods and then walk out and away, to Hatha-Yoga, psychic folly or lycergic acid?

When a builder builds he clears the ground for his new foundations. Then he sees that the basic structure will support the whole. Should we not also clear the mind—at least that part of it that we can reach—of the ruins of past thinking, before building our palace of Dharma which will one day reach the sky? Is Jesus' parable of the man who built his house on sand not apt to all of us?

The Burmese have a thousand years of Buddhism behind them; the Japanese have the same. Both are of the Orient. When Buddhism came to Europe it was by way of ideas, exciting, provocative ideas and utterly new values. The suggestion of meditation came much later. Let the mind be trained to obedience in order that the principles of rediscovered truth may form the foundation from which the previous ruins had been carefully removed. Counting the breaths is an excellent practice, for odd moments, for the walk to the bus, in the bus, and a thousand moments of the day. And then? Study, deep and deeper study, with the instrument of thought in which the West take pride, to understand and assimilate and practise and show forth the tremendous principles of basic Buddhism—the Three Signs, the Four Noble Truths, Karma and Rebirth and all the rest of them. When these become basic to our action, the main-spring of our daily life in thought and feeling, word and deed, is there not then time for spending long hours in this un-English practice? For the few it is right already; for the growing many, surely the Buddha's order is right; Basic Buddhism, then Sila in every moment of the day—*then* meditation.

What is it? 'Meditation,' says Dr Evans-Wentz in his Foreword to Miss Lounsbery's *Buddhist Meditation*, 'is the royal highway to man's understanding of himself.' This magnificent statement is profoundly true. In the words of a Buddhist Scripture, 'Cease to do evil; learn to do good; cleanse your own heart. This is the Teaching of the Buddhas.' First comes the dual process of abandoning wrong ways of thought and action, and developing those which reflect the One and are therefore 'right'. But then there opens the true and final Path, the assault on illusion, the illusion of self and all its works, for the life of morality is only a preparation for the ultimate reunion of mind with Mind. The Buddhist Goal is the full Enlightenment of the individual mind, a process wherein the light flows in as the man-made barriers of self are slowly cleared away. This process, as often pointed out, is not the salvation of a soul but the liberation of the Self from self, of the individual mind from the illusion of separation. The process of self-liberation is therefore confined to the individual mind, though carried out for the ultimate benefit of all. It follows that no task is more important to the Buddhist; all else, the acquiring of knowledge, moral improvement, and even the practice of 'right' action are secondary, and in themselves of no complete avail. The reason is obvious, for in Buddhist teaching, 'All that we are is the result of what we have thought; it is founded on our thoughts, it is made up of our thoughts'. In the cyclic process of becoming, mind is paramount, for it is the thoughts begotten in the mind which manifest as action, 'good' or 'bad', according as the act moves towards Oneness or away from it; when the thought is right, right action follows. The Buddhist Way, then, is a process of self-liberation of the individual mind, first by a thorough understanding of its basic principles, then of their application in morality or integrity of character, and finally in mind-expansion to enlightenment. But the factors need not be taken seriatim. All may be developed at the same time, and even at an early stage the planned, unceasing work of mental purification and expansion fills the working day. The methods used have varied in the schools of thought developed in the vast field of Buddhism. In the West, the technique of the Theravada was the first known, and it may be useful to give here an outline of its technique. The argument runs: All men are suffering, and suffering from the fires of lust, hatred and illusion. The fault is theirs, and arises from the illusion of self. As this illusion resides in the mind, the mind must be purified by a strenuous course of training which will destroy the illusion, and produce instead the conscious awareness of Reality in which there is Mind-Only and no self. This bhavana, or process of mental liberation, has two stages. The first is Sati-patthana, in which the mind is controlled, trained to see things as they are without emotion or thought of self, and prepared as a hand-wrought instrument for the final approach to Enlightenment. The second stage is to transcend the limitations of the instrument thus made. But only by mind can the mind be transcended, and there is no short-cut which avoids the early stages of the process; only through a controlled and well-developed mind can the final stage of No-mind, which is All-mind, be achieved. The spiritual insight or *Vipassana* so gained may be compared with the *Satori* of Zen, but the true relation between these and other exalted states of consciousness is a matter too advanced, and too debatable, to be considered here.

In the course of *Sati-patthana* the four *Jhanas,* advanced stages of consciousness, are reached and transcended, and various *Iddhis,* supernormal powers, are incidentally developed. All this is well set out in *The Heart of Buddhist Meditation,* by the Ven. Nyanaponika Thera, but a teacher is essential for this strenuous course of training, and the student wishing to use it should apply for the assistance which he needs.

In the West, the need for some guidance in mind-development was made acute some thirty years ago by a sudden spate of books which were, whatever the motive of their authors, dangerous in the extreme. No word was said in them of the sole right motive for mind-development, the enlightenment of the meditator for the benefit of all mankind, and the reader was led to believe that it was quite legitimate to study and practise mindfulness, and the higher stages which ensue, for the benefit of business efficiency and the advancement of personal prestige. In these circumstances *Concentration and Meditation,* a handbook written for the Western mind, was compiled and published by the Buddhist Society, with constant stress on the importance of right motive, and ample warning of the dangers, from a headache to insanity, which lie in wait for those who trifle with the greatest force on earth, the human mind. At the same time Miss Lounsbery, of Les Amis du Bouddhisme in Paris, published her *Buddhist Meditation in the Southern School,* stressing the same advice to beginners as given in our own more catholic work. Both books emphasize—for both are still in print—the need of practice, as distinct from theory; for as Dr Evans-Wentz pointed out in his Introduction to Miss Lounsbery's book, 'Buddhism emphasizes that the realization of Truth is incomparably more important than belief in Truth; that religious faith and devotion, being merely the first steps on the Path, are of themselves not enough; that if Truth is to be realized, there must be Right Belief, Right Intentions, Right Speech, Right Actions, Right Means of Livelihood, Right Endeavouring, Right Mindfulness, Right Meditation'. In other words, to use an old analogy, it is useless to sit in an armchair at a point whence a dozen roads lead off in various directions, and merely to consider the merits of each and the nature of the goal at the end of them. It is better to rise and tread the first steps along one of them than to consider the whole of them and to practise none. Indeed, so important is the need for practice in meditation that it has been said there are two rules for a new practitioner, 'Begin, and continue'! In the practice of both rules the quality of *tamas*, inertia, will strenuously resist the will. If it is hard to plan and to begin the long period of effort, it is far more difficult to continue, and only the early results, greater control of thought, serenity of mind and inner quietude persuade the beginner that the effects are worth the effort to produce the cause.

One of the earliest difficulties is the choice of English terms. *Samma Sati*, the seventh step on the Eightfold Path, is well translated as Right Mindfulness, but the eighth, *Samma* (or full) *Samadhi*, is often given as Right Concentration. In truth the term is untranslatable, but the three words used in *Concentration and Meditation* to describe the entire process are perhaps the most helpful and will here be used. Concentration is the creation of the instrument; meditation is the right use of it; contemplation transcends it. In the early stages, the first two should be kept separate, for different considerations apply; finally, all are merged in the One-Mind.

Concentration, which is a term far wider than 'attentiveness', an early stage of *Satipatthana*, certainly begins with the practice of attention, full, impersonal, objective attention to the task or thing in hand. All successful business men acquire this faculty, for without it the day's work is impossible. It is in no way 'spiritual', being only the power of sustained and directed thought. It is harder to turn the same faculty within. A man who is proud of his ability to concentrate in the presence of distraction will be quite unable to turn the searchlight of his thought on to the nature and process of his thinking. The West is extravert, its power turned on the nature and use of external forces, whether of money, politics or the Niagara Falls. The older East is essentially introvert, its values being sought within, and the criterion of value being the mind's expansion in understanding as distinct from the worldly power of the personality.

In either event the mind must be broken to harness and yoked to its owner's will, an immensely difficult task, as all who strive to focus thought on a chosen subject find. 'As a fletcher straightens his arrows, so the wise man straightens his unsteady mind, which is hard indeed to control.' From the choice of a subject which arises in the course of 'usual life', such as doing accounts, drafting an agreement or a complex piece of knitting, to a choice made for the sake of an exercise in self-control is a large step, and the mind jibs at it. At first the subject may be external, a rose, a distant view, or the door-knob; then a subjective object, *i.e.* a subject, will be taken. Breathing itself may be used, or the body as such, the emotions in their permutations, or the incredibly swift rise and fall of thoughts within the mind. Miss Lounsbery points out that interest helps the power to concentrate; it is only at a later stage that the power is developed to concentrate by an effort of will on something without interest or, and this is of more value, to find interest in that which is, in all the circumstances, the next thing to be done.

Only when the mind is trained to obedience, as a small dog may be trained to come to heel when called (and to stay there), is the student in a fit state to begin to meditate. Immediately new rules apply; new aspects of the laws of life begin to operate. The would-be saviour of himself and all mankind is moving ahead of his fellow men. He is developing powers not known to, much less possessed by those of his own intellectual standing. Just as magic is a knowledge of the laws of nature not yet possessed by 'scientists', much less by the common herd, so meditation quickly develops powers not yet possessed by the most efficient business man. Why, then, the teacher may ask the pupil, do you meditate, giving your time and thought and energy to mental development not yet achieved by most of your fellow men? It is vital that the answer be true and clear. There is one sole motive for self-advancement which is 'right', and it is not the aggrandizement of self. Indeed, as the inner development continues, the personality grows less, and with the withdrawal of energy from its worldly affairs may tend to fade out in the eyes of men. The sole motive for meditation is to purge the self of illusion, to develop the faculty of intuition to the point of Enlightenment, and to desire that Enlightenment, if desired at all, for the sake of the One-Mind. Anything less is evil, an abuse of powers, and the karma of such misuse is terrible. It is well to think long before beginning to meditate and to see that the reason for the vast new effort is 'right'.

For the first time physical habits become important. There are ample reasons for the right posture to be observed, for the time to be regular, and the place, if possible, the same. To strain is foolish, for the process must be slow, but if the practice is well conceived and regular, results will appear. Some of them will be unwelcome, and psychic visions and noises, emotional disturbances and alarming dreams may deter the would-be Arhat. The mental hindrances are worse. Miss Lounsbery mentions five: craving, ill will, sloth, agitated states of mind and doubt. I have myself found many more. But the rewards are commensurate. There is quietude of body, as of emotions, and the dying down of the fires of lust and hatred which burn so tediously within the mind. Thought is steadied, strengthened and increasingly brought under control. The newly acquired impersonality of thinking, with thoughts bereft of emotion and the constant reference to 'I', brings the clear light of a new serenity, and love acquires new meaning. It is compassion now which speaks, with the voice of the Silence, and provides the 'right' because un-selfish motive for every act.

This new affection for all fellow forms of life can be canalized in useful action. The four *Brahma Viharas*, for example, can be usefully exercised at any time and place, from the office to a restaurant, from a dentist's waiting-room to a bus. These four virtues, though powers of the mind is a better term, are Metta, loving-kindness or good-will, Karuna, compassion, Mudita, sympathetic joy, and Upekkha, equanimity of mind. In a famous quotation from a Buddhist Sutta, 'He lets his mind pervade one quarter of the world with thoughts of *metta*, with thoughts of *karuna*, with thoughts of *mudita* and with thoughts of *upekkha*; and so the second quarter, and so the third and so the fourth. And thus the whole wide world, above, below, around and everywhere does he continue to pervade with heart of love, compassion, joy and equanimity, far-reaching, great, beyond measure, free from the least trace of anger or ill-will.'

The subjects of meditation are all but infinite. All virtues may be used, and noble thoughts, for as Epictetus, the Greek slave, said, 'You must know that it is no easy thing for a principle to become a man's own, unless each day he maintain it and hear it maintained, as well as work it out in life'. And how shall it be better maintained and applied than in constantly meditating upon it? Any phrase will do from a thinker or poet who speaks the eternal Wisdom, and in *Concentration and Meditation* a few score suggestions are made. Some in the West object to a few of the practices of *Sati-patthana*, such, for example, as the meditations on a corpse or in a graveyard, designed to bring home the truth of *anicca*, change. Certainly, these are not suitable to the beginner, and are only mentioned here to remove the belief that Eastern meditation largely consists in such practices. They are in fact but a brief stage in the slow and complete withdrawal of the mind from sense attachment, and have their uses, as some of us even of the West well know.

But it is always easier to keep up the pressure in a long and graded task like mind-development if there is a definite course prescribed. There are many such in Buddhism, and the student should decide his own. Thereafter what matters is persistence, and the due effects will follow the unremitting pressure of the cause. The whole range of Sati-patthana, right mindfulness, is available to London students with competent instructors, but this, as all other systems of the Theravada, limits its ideals to the Arhat, the self-perfected individual who works for his own liberation in the belief that until he has purged his own mind from the snares of self he cannot usefully assist mankind. To a man or woman of the complementary temperament this cold, impersonal analysis, and subsequent training of the mind to the smooth efficiency of a beautiful machine, is insufficient to supply their total needs. The Mahayana range is wide and equally available, though the expert teachers may for the moment be hard to find. There is the ritual school of Japanese Shingon Buddhism, and the more tantric ritual of certain schools of Tibet is practised now in Europe. More easy to find, though hardest of all to practise, is the joyous, inconsequent and almost non-sensical technique of Zen, which aims at no less than sudden and immediate, direct Enlightenment, in flashes at first but later as a fully developed faculty of the mind. It would seem, though the point is debatable, that Zen technique should begin when the mind has already reached a fairly advanced stage of right mindfulness. Not until the intellect is well developed and controlled can it be transcended; yet until it is transcended the Absolute of the One Mind can never be truly known. To the extent that Zen has a specified ideal it shares the Bodhisattva doctrine of the Mahayana schools, but the man who is dedicated to the service of all life, and in particular to his fellow human beings, must still perfect himself if he wishes to be of better service than a vague goodwill, and the Arhat and the Bodhisattva ideals are complementary as the two sides of a coin.

From Concentration to Meditation, from Meditation to Contemplation, such are the stages, and of the third stage little can usefully be said. At this level of consciousness all words are slightly ridiculous. As is said in the *Lankavatara Sutra*, 'If you assert that there is such a thing as Noble Wisdom it no longer holds good, for anything of which something is asserted thereby partakes of the nature of being, and thus has the quality of birth. The very assertion, "All things are un-born", destroys the truthfulness of it.' For it is clear to the intellect that every statement is short of truth, for its opposite must, in the Absolute, be equally true. All pairs of opposites are relative, and only of value and meaning in a relative world. 'The Tao that can be expressed is not the eternal Tao', and descriptions of Nirvana, or the same experience by another name, are demonstrably untrue.

Contemplation, as I defined it in opening this section in *Concentration and Meditation*, 'is an utterly impersonal awareness of the essence of the thing observed'. When self is purged from the mind of the observer, the trinity of seer, seen and the seeing is dissolved, and the seer sees by becoming the essence of the thing observed. The operative word is essence, as distinct from the inessential form. For the essence of all things alike is *tathata*, the suchness of things, and this suchness is 'void' (*sunya*), of all particulars. Only a mind in the void is No-mind, resting in the state of no-thinking or Mu-shin, and only the mind that has reached such a stage for a second or an hour can speak—and he cannot speak of it—of the utter serenity and power that flows from Life itself into a mind that sets no barrier against its flow. But these are the fruits of *bhavana*, using the

term for meditation in its widest sense. The tree must grow from
an acorn to an oak before the fruit appears. First come the exercises, backed by right motive and an indomitable will; then the
right use of the new-won instrument. Only then comes the
nakedness of a mind new cleansed of its own self-wrought
illusion. This is freedom indeed, yet—asked by a pupil, 'Master,
how shall I free my mind?' the Master replied, 'Who puts you
under restraint?'

We Live in Boxes

We live in boxes, great or small, confined
In shapes and colours of our thought and will.
The measured ambit of each lidded mind
Scarce but a drop of wider thought lets spill
To blur the boasted label, loudly signed
With ownership, that to each suffered ill
Bears witness. Locked in self, to heaven blind
We fiercely cling to limitation still.

Oh for a sword, Manjusri's diamond blade
To split these weary walls, to slay all fond
Conviction, thought, belief and orthodoxies!
Oh for a moment of no-mind, afraid
Of no thing, deathless, bursting every bond
Of me in otherness . . .

                   We live in boxes.

Deeper Truths of Buddhism

15

Conversion in Buddhism

Much has been written on conversion, for the subject is of perennial fascination to all who study religious history and experience. It fascinates because the experience is in essence irrational, and therefore unsettling to the pigeon-holing minds of Western orthodoxy. Most that is written, however, concerns religious conversion, in the Christian sense of the word religion. As such it has, generally speaking, three characteristics. It is predominantly emotional; it is devotional, in the sense that it pertains to Bhakti Yoga, the way of devotion to a beloved and personified Ideal; and it is theistic, being concerned with a Personal God, which is the most common form of the personified ideal.

The Buddhist conversion is different. As Professor D. T. Suzuki says, 'the general tendency of Buddhism is more intellectual than emotional, and its doctrine of Enlightenment distinguishes it sharply from the Christian view of salvation'.[1] He goes on to point out, however, that the intellect in Buddhism is of the transcendental order, 'which does not issue in logical dualism'. On the contrary, it works for synthesis, for the awareness in which duality has ceased to exist. In Buddhist philosophy 'all distinctions are falsely imagined', and the 'heresy of separateness' between the part and the whole is the cause of the illusion of a separate self, and hence of the omnipresence of suffering. Buddhist conversion, therefore, is the dispersal of an illusion, the dissolution of a mental fog which lets the sun shine through.

[1] *Essays in Zen Buddhism*. First Series, p. 217.

The Buddhist experience of *Satori*, the goal of Zen experience, is described as the 'opening of the mind-flower', or 'the removing of the bar'. The experience thus takes place at a higher level than the emotional release of Christian conversion, for the former pertains to Jnana Yoga, the way of wisdom, as distinct from that of Bhakti Yoga, of devotion to Someone other than oneself, or of 'right action', the Karma Yoga described in the Bhagavat Gita.

The Buddhist conversion is a turning to a new point of view, towards a light by which the darkness of the Unconscious is illumined to a greater awareness. It is primarily concerned with a revelation of the more True rather than the more Good, with greater wisdom rather than with greater morality. Hence there is much, at the moment of conversion, of 'Now I see', or 'Now the Way is clear to me'; there is little if anything of 'Now I will abandon the sins of the flesh and develop the nobler virtues'. To the Buddhist, morality follows awareness, the lessening of *avidya*, ignorance, whereas greater awareness is not a necessary consequence of improved morality. As the womb and essence of that great system of development known as Buddhism is the Enlightenment of the All-Enlightened One, it follows that in Buddhism the pursuit of enlightenment has supreme priority.

These differences are not of wording only. Buddhism, it must be stressed, denies the existence of the Christian's Personal yet Almighty God. The nearest equivalent, as the prime emanation of THAT, the Namelessness, is the concept of Mind-only which, being utterly impersonal, is quite unsuited for human devotion. Much follows from the difference. In the absence of a mighty Being who has power to withhold the sequence of cause-effect the Buddhist looks within for his spiritual needs, including his 'salvation'. He is therefore at the outset of his religious life thrown back on his own interior resources; for him the Buddha is never more, though never less, than a Guide and Leader on the Way along which in the end each blade of grass will find deliverance.

The Buddhist and the religious approach to conversion have, however, this in common, that both attempt to transcend duality. Religious conversion produces a link with 'God' in which the Beloved and the worshipper are one. Even Western psychology is concerned with the integration of the individual, however that term be construed. Yet only Buddhism, and the Zen School of Buddhism, to which the existence of a Personal Almighty God is quite unknown, is primarily concerned with the deliberate development of an awareness which is beyond discrimination, beyond the sense of duality of this and that, even beyond the awareness of difference, save in function, between any of the 'Pairs of Opposites' or indeed between any two 'compounded things'.

All comparisons, however, to be of any use, must distinguish at an early stage two paths of self-development, that which leads towards conversion, and the far more strenuous and 'narrow way' from the moment of conversion to the final Goal. The first has a thousand semblances by which the feet of men have reached the same Gate by their own efforts and their own free will. This Gate is the first 'initiation' when, as the Buddhists say, 'the stream is entered'. Thereafter there are further moments of achieved development until, through steadily progressive trials and triumphs, the 'further shore' is attained. This moment of deliberate entry on a path to utter self-annihilation which is yet a Self-perfection is irrevocable.

As I have written elsewhere:

> The future lies unmoulded in my hands;
> A path winds out before.
> There is no backward way. Behind me stands
> A closéd door.

Yet the two paths, that which leads to conversion and that which leads therefrom to the final goal, are in essence one. 'I am the Way, the Truth and the Life,' said Jesus, the Christ, and the same applies to the Christ-Buddhic principle inherent in every mind. 'Thou canst not travel on the Path before thou hast become that Path itself," says *The Voice of the Silence*. All is here and now, and the beginning and the end of the journey lies within. Conversion at the entry of the Path and Enlightenment at the end are indeed two parts of a single process beyond the limitations of time.

What, then, is conversion in Buddhist eyes? It is not a mere

H

change of interest, however sudden, as a man may turn on retirement from banking to gardening, or from travel to the study of philosophy. Nor is it one end of the mental swing of those who suffer from the manic-depressive psychosis. It is not partial, as with a sudden emotional release in a man whose mind has long been pent within the confines of intellectual thought. Rather it is a reorientation of the whole man to a new purpose from a new point of view. The same things are seen but henceforth they are seen differently.

The cause of the change is the release of a new force in the mind, and the release only comes when pressure has been deliberately built up to a point where something must give way. That which gives way is the opposition, the block in the pipe of the stream of life, the cloud which obscures the sun. As Dr Suzuki says of *Satori*, there must be 'accumulation, saturation, explosion', and the experience involves not only the part which is striving but the whole man. First comes the frontal attack with every energy concentrated at a single point. The 'searching and contriving', as it is called, reaches an impasse. Whatever the problem, the 'hopeless' situation, or the fragment of the Wisdom not yet understood, the whole will must be bent upon the solution, and only when all available strength has been exhausted does the new source suddenly, amazingly, 'miraculously' appear.

When it comes it is unmistakable. As Jung points out, 'Religious experience is absolute. It is indisputable. No matter what the world thinks about religious experience, the one who has it possesses the great treasure of a thing that has provided him with a source of life, meaning and beauty and that has given a new splendour to the world and to mankind.'[1] For this purpose the Buddhist conversion is a religious experience. Dr Suzuki, as one would expect, says the same thing more succinctly: 'The opening of *satori* is the remaking of life itself.'[2]

The essence of conversion is in the turning. Psychologically, it is a process of intro-version, or turning inward, a withdrawal of consciousness from the phenomenal world into the noumenal Essence of Mind which is the highest cognizable Reality. 'Till now we have worked from the outside on what is within; now

---

[1] *Psychology and Religion*, C. G. Jung, pp. 1 and 3.
[2] *Essays in Zen Buddhism*, I, p. 217.

we tarry in the centre and rule what is external.'[1] The same principle is found in the Sutra of Hui-Neng, the 6th Patriarch of Zen Buddhism. Discussing the recitation of the Sutras he said, 'Whether Sutra-reciting will enlighten you or not depends on yourself. He who recites the Sutra with the tongue and puts its teaching into practice with his mind "turns round" the Sutra. He who recites it without putting it into practice is "turned round" by the Sutra.'[2] This turning about is a change of direction, from moving away from the light to a turning towards the light now suddenly re-seen. To the theist, it may be 'God-intoxication', to the poet, as in Thompson's poem, 'The Hound of Heaven', it is being overtaken by the divine arms of love. To the mystic, it is a joyous surrender to the will of God, the actual knowledge that 'I and my Father are one'. To the Buddhist it is the awareness of oneness. 'Look within—thou *art* Buddha', and with the looking the truth is seen.

The Buddhist doctrine is best found in the Lankavatara Sutra, in a way the most important of all Mahayana Buddhist texts. As summarized by Dr Suzuki in his *Studies in the Lankavatara Sutra*, 'To attain Nirvana, which is a state of emptiness (*sunyata*) inherent in the nature of things, and which again is a state of self-realization obtained by means of supreme wisdom (*arya-jnana*), there must be a revulsion (*paravritti*) at the deepest seat of consciousness known as the Alayavijnana'.[3] This deepest seat of consciousness is difficult to describe. It is clearly a key term in Buddhist philosophy, for it is at once the depository of all past karma and the womb of consequence to come. All differentiated forms of consciousness, including those of the five senses, arise from this mental receptacle, where all the memory of one's past deeds and psychic activities is deposited and preserved in a form of energy called Vasana (habit-energy). As the centre of the 'revulsion' or conversion, it is clearly comparable to the border-line between the unconscious and the conscious mind on which, according to Dr Jung, the new Self as an integrating awareness must be born. In one sense, then, it is a Universal Consciousness, containing the past and future and the energy of both; in

[1] *The Secret of the Golden Flower*, Wilhelm and Jung, p. 60.
[2] *The Sutra of Hui-Neng*, p. 77.
[3] p. 128.

another, it is the springboard of individual action and becoming. It is near enough to the heart of things for all external circumstance to be seen from it as 'mind-born' from the womb of Mind-only; on the other hand, it destroys the domination of the separative forms of consciousness, and restores the central vision to the common ground between the universal and individual fields of consciousness.

The importance of the Alaya consciousness is that like the 'Essence of Mind' in the Sutra of Hui-neng, it is 'intrinsically pure'. The revulsion, therefore, is a process of shaking off the defilements of illusion until the ever-existent Light of non-duality is once more seen. Hence Dr Suzuki's description of *paravritti* as an opening which must be made to the non-discriminative and transcendental intellect, wherein and by which all is known as one.[1]

In terms of Buddhist metaphysics, the turning takes place when the descending consciousness or spirit reaches the nadir of matter and turns home again. The Universe, unrolled into matter, turns in the fullness of unimaginable time and begins to roll up again. 'As above, so below', and the same process takes place in each unit of evolving life. But whereas when the spirit was descending into matter the law of selfishness, of increasing self-expression through the self, was 'right', now the self must be shed as a cocoon unwound, and the consequent new strain is intense. For the units of life of which the bodies of man are composed are still going down into matter. The integrating unit of consciousness which is now, in full awareness, beginning to rise, is at war with the desires of its descending parts and principles. The consequent tension must increase as the new man gains impetus in his strenuous climb to the light. This may in part explain why all who take their own development in hand immediately suffer a host of ills, physical, emotional and mental, comparable at times with those of Job. It may be his own 'evil' karma which the efforts of the new-born climber calls down on his head, but the cause of the avalanche is his own deliberate movement, and he has no right to complain of the consequence.

The moment of conversion is a turning to face the 'shadow', as Dr Jung describes it, 'the other aspect' of our conscious mind

[1] Ibid., p. 185.

116

which provides the necessary tension in the field of consciousness. This opposite pole in the bi-polar field, the other end of the swing of the pendulum, is linked with the complex of opposing forces which together make up the individuality of the human being concerned. Conversion occurs when the shadow, the 'dark brother' which personifies the suppressed or yet unconscious material of the total mind, is bravely and deliberately faced. 'Everyone carries a shadow,' says Dr Jung, 'and the less it is embodied in the individual's conscious life, the blacker and deeper it is.'[1] So long as it is unconscious it cannot be corrected or assimilated. It follows that the conscious man is unconsciously ill-balanced, and his self-presentation to the world is a lie to his fellow man and, which is far more important for his mental health, a lie to himself. So long as it is repressed and isolated the 'shadow' is liable to burst forth in moments of unawareness, to the embarrassment of the mind concerned and the bewilderment of his friends.

Not knowing of this other self, which is the Mr Hyde to every thought and act of the would-be Dr Jekyll, the individual projects the contents of his mind onto outside forces, people, and things. These factors, be it the weather, the Government, his stars or his wife, are blamed for his own shortcomings and irritation, and the process of integration of the patient, whether or not he yet considers himself as such, is the deliberate withdrawal of these projections, one by one, until the mind as a whole can stand on its own feet, as it is and no better. It is not hard for the intellect to appreciate, for example, that 'By oneself evil is done; by oneself one suffers. By oneself evil is left undone; by oneself one is purified'; or that, 'Though one man conquer a thousand times a thousand men in battle, he who conquers himself is the greatest warrior'; or that, in brief, 'You yourself must make the effort. (Even) Buddhas do but point the Way.' Yet for these magnificent sayings from the Dhammapada to be 'actualized', made real by conscious application to the moment's affairs, is a rare and wonderful turning about in consciousness. And he is a brave man who succeeds in doing it. As Dr Jung points out, 'We are still swamped with projected illusions. If you imagine someone who is brave enough to withdraw these projections, all and

[1] *Psychology and Religion,* p. 93.

sundry, then you get an individual conscious of a pretty thick shadow. Such a man has saddled himself with new problems and conflicts. He has become a serious problem to himself, as he is now unable to say that *they* do this or that, *they* are wrong and *they* must be fought against. He lives in the "house of self-collection". Such a man knows that whatever is wrong in the world is in himself, and if he only learns to deal with his own shadow then he has done something real for the world. He has succeeded in removing an infinitesimal part at least of the unsolved gigantic problems of our day.'[1] Only in the 'house of self-collection' ('mindful and self-possessed', as the Buddhist Scriptures have it) is the individual fit to 'walk on', or to enter the stream of which the further shore is Enlightenment. As Epictetus, the Stoic slave, remarked, 'If any man be unhappy let him know that it is by reason of himself alone'. This is a brave discovery. It is the awareness of the Buddhist doctrine of karma, that 'all that we are is the result of what we have thought', and that no man is to blame for what we are, or think, or feel, or do, but we ourselves who made us so.

If an intellectual understanding of these principles does not suffice to cause the 'revulsion' at the seat of consciousness, it follows that the pivotal point of turning, as it were, is in a higher faculty. This, as already described, is *buddhi*, the intuition, for only *buddhi* can integrate the opposites of Self and shadow, the conscious and unconscious mind. Only *buddhi*, higher than emotion and intellect, can reach the experience of transcending the difference of the opposites; only *buddhi*, the faculty of *bodhi*, the wisdom of Enlightenment, can provide the flame which, fully roused, can burn out self and leave but Self to pursue its own high destiny.

But before the faculty of *buddhi* can be properly developed the intellect, trained to its full capacity, must be deliberately transcended. Few with considerable mental powers are aware that the intellect knows nothing; it knows but about. In many it is a mould of iron, of cast iron with our Western education of perpetual fact; of wrought iron in the few who train their own minds as controllable instruments. Now the mould must be broken, the limitations of conceptual thought perceived. In most

[1] Ibid., p. 101.

of us, while the intellect is surfeited with fact the heart is starved of meaning. We must therefore break the concrete roof of rational thought and allow the light to enter. We must climb the ladder of sense to its utmost limits and then, with a laugh, jump off into the void of non-sense which is found on arrival to be true. This needs courage, yet only in the Void is fullness; only where there is no-thing is everything worth having to be found.

Although the existence of the intuition is well known to Western psychology, its deliberate development as an independent faculty is easier for the Eastern student than for his Western brother. For the East and West are complementary in development, as Dr Abegg has so brilliantly described in *The Mind of East Asia*. The Western intellect or 'thought-machine' works in a straight line, as with the logical development of given premises. The Eastern mind approaches with an encircling movement, regarding the object simultaneously from many points of view. This 'total thinking', however, is possible without the thinker noticing the conflict in the logical anomalies and even absurdities involved. For the East is more intuitively developed and despises much of the West's insistence on the differences revealed by intellectual analysis. Even the classification of mental processes, by which we carefully distinguish philosophy, psychology, religion, metaphysics, morality and many more, as utterly distinct though allied fields, is meaningless to the Eastern student of the total man.

Yet within this subdivided field of mental endeavour the intuition is given by common consent the sole power of 'direct' awareness. The intellect knows 'about', and it may be a great deal about, a particular subject. Only *buddhi*, the mind's inherent faculty of *bodhi*, ultimate wisdom, *knows*. Yet between the unillumined and completely illumined intellect there are of course all possible gradations, and at what precise point of the mind's illumining the total man 'turns over' to the path of return it is difficult to say. The moment of conversion may be in truth a series of movements which are the culmination of a long process of interior growth. The effect may be sudden, yet the cause may be the effect of a long period of effort in the deeps of mind. For a while there will be flashes from the unconscious of a glory soon to be seen, and by these flashes of a newborn light all heaven and earth will be seen as with new eyes. Previous tension will be relieved and followed by the building up of new; the previous code of mental and moral values will be utterly revised. The flashes of light will inevitably fade; doubt will replace a blinding certainty. But something has happened, something so deep, so fundamental, that it may be a long while before the outward man is changed. For the change is at the centre, and only when the time is ripe will a new man, utterly 're-born', appear.

The conversion may come at any age and in either sex, for the experience is not understandable without the doctrine of rebirth. Such profound 'revulsion' at the seat of consciousness is never the outcome of an hour's thought, still less of the intellect's acceptance of a doctrine heard, it may be, for the first time. It is the reward of a process which has lasted many lives. It may come in adolescence, when the awakening mind is faced with the choice between God and Mammon, the way of the spirit and the way of the world; or it may come at the change of middle age, when the claims of the flesh are less importunate. But whenever it comes it is indeed a second birth. Verily, 'except a man be born again he cannot see the kingdom of God', and the 'kingdom of God' is within.

The effect of conversion is profound. It brings no pride. 'He who is puffed up by the slightest impression, "I am now enlightened" is no better than he was when under delusion.'[1] There is an awareness of expansion, of serenity, of certainty as to the Goal and the way to it, but no pride; for the self which boasted of the self's achievement died in the process of new birth. The change is comparable to the sudden descent of the other of a pair of scales. Formerly selfishness and thoughts of 'I' weighed heavily. Then came the balance-point of doubt; now self-lessness, the awareness of a universal Self has won the day. There is a conscious shift in the polarity of tension from the self to the Self. The scope of understanding is indefinitely widened. A Plan is seen in the universal becoming, although there is no Planner. The law of cycles is for the first time found to be a working and usable reality. Henceforth the pilgrim is increasingly able to ascend, as it were, to the bridge of his own ship,

[1] *The Sutra of Hui-Neng,* p. 84.

and to direct its total movement to a given end. And that which takes control is the same power which aforetime lacked the power to command. There may be truth in Dr Jung's[1] description of some 'other' influence which is felt to have taken over the control of one's activity. Yet it is the raising of habitual consciousness to a new height and therefrom a new vision, as it might be that of a lighthouse keeper who climbs through stage after stage to approach the Light. And the analogy is not less true if the keeper finds himself suddenly shot up in a lift!

Henceforth Buddhism is found to be the unfolding of the Buddhist life and not the study of recorded doctrine. The Goal is clear and single, Enlightenment, and this involves the domination of duality, the perpetual awareness of One-only at all moments of the day. Henceforth the truth is commensurate with the way, wisdom with the process of development. Belief and its application are seen as the two sides of a coin. 'The whole of the Buddhist life is not in merely seeing into the truth, but in living it, experiencing it, so that there will be no dualism in one's life of seeing and living; seeing must be living, and living seeing, with no hiatus between them, except in language.'[2]

Thereafter the way is filled with joy and filled with suffering, and the paradox must be proved. For this, the *via dolorosa* of all mystical description, demands a degree of concentrated effort which must be expected and endured when the sacrifice upon the altar is no less than self, the self which nearly all men fondly regard as 'I'. Only later dawns the awareness of a brotherhood of sacrifice, whose brothers know that 'there is no such thing as sacrifice; there is only opportunity to serve'. Suffering is seen as the outward effects of an inner process of purification. The adjustments in the mind are a cleansing of the impurities of illusion. The self suffers and complains, yet the only end to suffering is the death of that which suffers, self and its desires. The still small voice of Bodhicitta, the wisdom-heart, is now a factor in all conscious functioning; the light of compassion, once perceived, may be dimmed with the mists of illusion but will never be utterly put out. As the last of the fetters are one by one destroyed, by the positive process of attack and destruction or

[1] Foreword to Dr Suzuki's *Introduction to Zen Buddhism*, p. 17.
[2] *Studies in the Lankavatara Sutra*, p. 105.

the negative Zen technique of letting them fall with a gentle chuckle and a cup of tea, the final stages of the Eightfold Path are successively attained. Thereafter is mystery, for the finite mind can never describe the infinite. Men glibly talk about Nirvana, but 'the Tao that can be described is not the eternal Tao', and the same applies to its goal. It is enough that the Great Ones have, at the portals of this inconceivable bliss, turned back, with a new conversion, back to reduce that 'sea of sorrow, formed of the tears of men', and to set their feet upon the Way proclaimed by the All-Compassionate One, their Master. We too who seek conversion will in time be called upon to choose between bliss and the service of our fellow men. Says *The Voice of the Silence*, 'The first step is to live to benefit mankind'. And why? The answer is clear. 'Now bend thy head and listen well, O Bodhisattva—Compassion speaks and saith: "Can there be bliss when all that lives must suffer? Shalt thou be saved and hear the whole world cry?"'

16

Beyond God

The religious man—for whom the ultimate Goal is the sole purpose of life and each moment of it—is rare, and always will be. More numerous, though few compared with the world's unnumbered millions, are the seekers of Reality who, bored with the average life of comfort and unthinking mind, look elsewhere, vaguely or intensely, for knowledge of the Beyond of sense-experience. Most of these look about them, into books and articles, in groups and classes, into words and phrases caught they know not where. Few look up. Yet is not Aldous Huxley right? 'Is the house of the soul a mere bungalow with a cellar? Or does it have an upstairs above the ground floor of consciousness as well as a garbage-littered basement beneath?' We know so much now of this garbage-littered basement of the unconscious mind, and our dissociation from the shadow-self is, or so one hears in bright talk over the tea-cups, all but complete. What then? Is the world above so empty that those who have, or so they believe, discarded God are fearful to look up?

God as a name is dying on man's lips, and as a force, the force of Life itself, is fading from his heart. Maybe the sky is empty now, of the Light which lighteth the world, of the strength whence cometh our help. Yet God is only a name for Good, and another name for Beauty, Wisdom, Love. Are all these dying too, with the capital letters with which one used to spell them? Is Science, the new God of the machine, a jealous God that will have none other worshipped by his devotees? Has it become untrue to say—to feel, to know—that 'God's in His heaven— All's right with the world'?

Not for the Buddhist. In the Theravada School most emphasis is laid on the non-existence of the ever-changing self, the ego or shadow of modern psychology. There is indeed no abiding self in this or in any of its parts. But has any religious leader since the world began proclaimed no Self beyond the ego, no Self at all? Not the Buddha, who refused in terms to make any such statement. On the contrary, it is written in the scriptures of this very school that he proclaimed, 'There is, O Bhikkhus, an Unborn, a Not-become, a Not-made, a Not-compounded. If there were not, O Bhikkhus, this Unborn, Not-become, Not-made, Not-compounded, there could not be any escape from what is born, become, made, compounded. But since there is this Unborn, there is an escape from what is born.'

In the Northern, or Mahayana School, later in formation but to some minds deeper in its knowledge of the human heart, is the recognition of the vast bi-polar field of the Unborn in manifestation; of absolute and relative truth, of deathless Life and perishable form, of a self and a Not-self which is Self, awareness of which is in any man the state of Nirvana. This is the above of what is below, the inner unseen of what is visible without, the doctrine of the heart which sings aloud when the head has nothing more to say. This is the God who is still in his heaven, the mask or semblance of God-head, as Eckhart called it; the Parabrahman, as the Hindus call it; the Void, or Adi-Buddha or Dharma-kaya or Alaya-Vijnana as schools of the Buddhists call it, which is beyond all differences, all attributes, all names.

Then what is man? A compound of the Unborn and the born, say Buddhists, a thing of matter with a spark of that Light within him which, when fully seen will be the light of Nirvana. Matter itself is illusion, say the Buddhists, and all time spent in feeding its desires is waste of time which might be better spent on clearing away the veils of illusion from the Light. Matter is an appearance only; it is not, and science has proved at least this much of Buddhism. 'All form is emptiness, all emptiness is form.' Man as all else is a compound of life and form, spirit and matter, the Unborn manifesting in a ceaseless flux of the birth and death of form. Each form is everlastingly in movement, from birth, through development, to decay and death—of the form. Why, then, cherish it; why spend the cycle of the body's life subservient to its comfort and its pain-producing, low desires? Is this the purpose of Life, the will of the Unborn which ceaselessly in-forms each form or body, of man or mountain, planet or idea? Or is it to become what we are, to know that we are already enlightened, to break through, by one means or another, the limitations of the relative, and to know, beyond all argument of thought, that 'I and my Father are one', that the part may know, 'in this very body six feet in length', that it and the Whole, the not-self and the Self, are Not-two, not different.

The brain must learn this; the heart already knows. The intellect would give it a specific name, but the East ignores our Western-coined distinctions. We talk of philosophy, psychology, religion, mysticism and much beside. The East is content to study the human mind and its relation to All-Mind. If this be mysticism, it is older than the term. To the mystic of all times and places the Absolute is within, and he has seen, albeit in a moment's glimpse, its Light. 'Look within—thou *art* Buddha,' says *The Voice of the Silence*. Here is the Paramatman of Hinduism, the SELF beyond all separate thoughts of selfhood; here is the 'Spirit' of St Paul. But it is not an 'immortal soul', for there is no such thing; there can be no separate self in a world in which there are no two things which are separate from each other.

But if the Unborn is within it is also without. Nirvana is in Samsara, the world of becoming, of every day, or it is nowhere at all. For just as we learn from the 'Wisdom which has gone beyond' that 'all form is emptiness, all emptiness is form', so Nirvana *is* Samsara; Samsara *is* Nirvana, and both are aspects of the Unborn THAT which is nameless and must remain so.

Is all this theory only, 'views' to be discussed in class-rooms and debate? If so it is a thing external, alien from the springs of life, the forces which give purpose to the will. To the Buddhist it is more than views, even 'right views'. It is the vision of Reality, the direct tremendous seeing of things as they are which drives each part to renewed awareness that it is, and has never ceased to be the Whole. For Buddhism is a way of life, and a Buddhist is one who treads it. No doctrine has validity and force until it is applied. A Buddhist truth is a phrase without meaning until it has been found to be true by personal experience. A

Buddhist must become aware, in full unfettered consciousness:

That the Unborn is in each thing born:

That the light of Enlightenment shines in every circumstance and situation in the world of Samsara, of every day;

That joy and love and beauty unbounded shine and sing with unbelieving splendour in the darkest night of our unhappy minds;

That the God-head, or the Absolute, or the Buddha-mind are all the time in heaven, *and* in hell, and about and around and within us everywhere;

That 'It's all right', all of it, whether or not we approve of it, or think it right or wrong.

Let the pedant write this off as mysticism. Is it the less true? For the mystic knows the beyond of thought, and none shall take that awareness from him. He is little concerned with the world of duality, with science or morality, with the mind's mechanics of psychology, or with exercises for its control and development. These are of relative truth, on the valley floor of consciousness. On the uplands of enlightenment are the heights of metaphysics, the intuitive flashes which come in poetry, music, meditation, and to the greatest minds in any field. These moments of the nobler mind have this in common, that they lift, expand, reveal; they move from the edge to the centre, from the knowledge of the brain to the wisdom of the heart, from the sense of separation to self-identity.

This is a long journey, and few of us are in the foothills of this climb. There are sign-posts, but fog and doubt are all about us. Yet we know beyond reasoning that the Unborn waits our awareness, 'that all distinctions are falsely imagined', that there is THAT beyond both darkness and the Light, the Real and unreal, the illusion of death and the illusion of Immortality. 'If all things return to the One, to what does the One return?' asked a Zen master. We shall know the answer when we know that we know it, and have but to look and see.

Meanwhile how dreary is the present Western mind? Its values are exclusively material. Science, psychology, economics, even social science, all are material, unspiritual, aiming but at the body's comfort and its maintenance for the maximum number of years. Who stands up in the market place, or on the office floor to shout of the Unborn everywhere, of the Light which shines for those with open eyes? Who treads the Path to it, and sings each moment of the Way? Who lives as if Rebirth were true, and we had all time to plan the journey? Who accepts and uses karma as the universal law, by which 'to shatter this sorry scheme of things entire'; and then, 'remould it nearer to the heart's desire'? Does it matter so much if the body be comfortable if the spirit be singing like a bird within? Does it *matter* if feelings be hurt, our importance unappreciated, our minds unhappy with lamentation and despair?

We must be unhappy, for Life is one, and all who suffer share the burden of their suffering with all mankind. 'Compassion speaks and saith: "Can there be bliss when all that lives must suffer? Shalt thou be saved and hear the whole world cry?"' But 'If weeping may endure for a night, joy cometh in the morning', and the morning is now, and here, and doing this.

The Beyond is beckoning, that Wisdom which has gone beyond, that 'Light which never was on land or sea' which glows with a splendour which no worldly cares, nor Godless folly of a closed, 'agnostic' mind, can quench. How shall we find it? There is no need to seek! We may look for it with study and deliberate thought; with fierce endeavour and indomitable will; with laughter and non-sense which makes a fool of reasoning. Yet it is here all the time, in the thought and feeling of the moment, in the job in hand. We have but to live life as life lives itself, and in the process shout for the joy of living, or cry if we wish, or both at once, but never, never cease to be aware that God's in His heaven still. And beyond God? Need we go so far? As George Borrow delicately pointed out, 'Life is sweet, brother. There's night and day, brother, both sweet things; sun, moon and stars, brother, all sweet things; there's likewise a wind on the heath.'

In Search of Nothing

Why look for it? Why seek it? Why demand
Of each unravelled semblance this one thing
Which none has seen nor yet can understand?
We crave possession, comfortless; we cling
To blind enquiry, hope that in some phrase
Or virgin book or teacher's mouthing mind
The hot hand of pursuit, in sudden blaze
Of splendour will magnificently find
And hold it to the heart forever . . .
                                       Fools!
It is, and is not found or bought or given.
Effort, enquiry, search, these are the tools
Of revelation. Not in earth or heaven
Shall self, my self, ravish the final veil
And, kneeling, see the face which has no face
To see with, nor self-purpose to prevail.
Yet in that moment when the hands of space
Close to the compass of a point, not here
Not there, and time sleeps uninvented . .
                                      So,
The senses shall not find it anywhere.
'It lies within.' Oh clouded saying, No!
What of the host without if this within
Is sole and royal servant of the Light?
Is earth we know a darkened wheel of sin,
And heaven alone the dim-illumined height?

It lives and moves. It changes not. It is,
Within without, to all men visible.
In laughter, love and in our vanities
It is, divided, indivisible.
It is beyond, and more. It has no being,
No hands of action, no disturbing will.
It sees and knows, yet no thing sees in seeing.
It is the whole of all yet each thing still.
It shines in no-self-ness, in right endeavour
Fades when the one is falsely rent in two.
It waits, a moment stretched into forever,
Far, far beyond the reach of me or you.

Why seek it, then, in market place or mind?
Let it be lived and loved and deep enjoyed;
It is, we are, with nothing left behind.
How rich it is that owns and is the Void!

17

New Relationships

The search for Enlightenment brings new relationships, to reality, to circumstance, and to our fellow beings.

Buddhists are often labelled atheists, and if the God in whom they do not believe is the Almighty and yet personal Creator of popular Christian theology, the charge is rightly laid. The Buddhist teaching on Reality is clear. On the one hand, 'there is, O Bhikkus, an unborn, Unoriginated, Uncreated, Unformed. Were there not this Unborn, Unoriginated, Uncreated, Unformed, there would be no escape from the world of the born, the originated, the created, the formed.' But of this Ultimate Absolute nothing whatsoever can be said. Any attribute ascribed denies its opposite, and in the Absolute all attributes alike exist and are consumed. A God who is absolutely loving and good is also absolutely hating and bad. The very concept of totality implies a condition above and beyond all opposites, and it follows with inexorable logic that about such an Absolute nothing at all can be said. Hence the 'noble silence' of the Buddha on all questions touching the ultimate Reality. In the opening words of the Tao Te Ching, 'the Tao that can be expressed is not the eternal Tao', and the Buddhist practice is to lower the eyes from such unhelpful, meaningless abstractions to the task in hand, namely, treading the Way to Enlightenment.

Viewing man from the human end of the scale, the Buddhist believes in men made perfect, whether known as Rishis, Arhats, Bodhisattvas, Mahatmas or merely the Brothers. These, when they pass beyond the sphere of dull mortality, appear, clothed in the added robes of symbol and mythology, as gods indeed. But the human love of personification is not content to deify the most advanced of men. The ever-descending aspects of the Namelessness, the ineffable First Principle, are also deified. Aspects of Mind, they appear with bewildering names and attributes in all mythology, and it was left to modern psychologists like C. G. Jung to explain that, even when haughtily banished to the limbo of superstition, they reappear, more powerful because unrecognized, as aspects of the Unconscious which surrounds each human mind.

But between these gods and the Absolute there is, in the Buddha-Dharma, no one Being who is the conscious Creator of the Universe, who is both absolute and personal, Almighty God and Saviour of Mankind. In the esoteric tradition there are memories of men even greater than the four named Buddhas of the present cycle. If there was such a one who, at the dawn of the present era taught to infant humanity the ABC of the Way, some memory of his love and all but immeasurable wisdom may have lingered on, and be the prototype of the Almighty God beloved of theist religions. Yet even he, however Godlike, is not God. The same applies to the great ones of the Deva kingdom, that parallel evolution of 'Thrones, Dominations and Powers', angels and nature spirits of high and low degree, of which only the western scientist seems ignorant. In the famous Letter X of *The Mahatma Letters to A. P. Sinnett*, the Master who signed himself K.H. sets out in detail for his pupil's benefit the esoteric Buddhist tradition on the nature of Reality and man. Therein he writes:

'Our doctrine knows no compromises. It either affirms or denies, for it never teaches but that which it knows to be the truth. Therefore, we deny God both as philosophers and Buddhists. We know there are planetary and other spiritual lives, and we know there is in our system no such thing as God, either personal or impersonal. The word God was invented to designate the unknown cause of these effects which man has either admired or dreaded without understanding them, and since we claim, and that we are able to prove what we claim—i.e. the knowledge of that cause and causes—we are in a position to claim there is no God or Gods behind them.'

Of God, then, the Buddhists say that concerning the Ultimate All there is nothing to be said worth saying, and that the lesser gods are but aspects of the One Life in manifestation, in no sense absolute and themselves servants of the Law. If this be atheism, Buddhists are atheists; meanwhile in a theist country they pay respect to the national God, however named, and then pursue their God-less but tremendous Way to the heart's enlightenment.

How much nobler is the concept of one Life or Force which moves within the universal law to its own perfection. Biology accepts the unity of life in its own sphere of action; philosophy, in the Japanese Kegon school, describes it in the teaching of Jijimuge; mystics of whatever land and time speak in the identical symbols of the same God-life within. Who doubts that life is one, and yet how few can face the implications of this fact? In pure philosophy, the doctrine of Jijimuge, 'the unimpeded interdiffusion of all particulars', transcends the grandeur even of the Vedas and Upanishads of India. 'Thou art THAT' was a noble cry, proclaiming the absolute identity of the part and the whole. Only one step further was possible, and the Japanese Buddhists took it over a thousand years ago. Not only is the manifested part and the Absolute Whole triumphantly conceived as one, but the parts are one with each other. As I said in *Zen Buddhism*, 'According to Jijimuge all "thou's", or apples or boats, are not only THAT but *directly* each other, completely and altogether. Two points on the circumference of a circle, instead of merely looking to the self-same centre, *are* at the centre all the time . . . '

How far beyond the concept of a personal and sentimental God is this sublime conception. And the mystics, even of theist countries, speak of a Beloved who is never more than a warm personification of the Infinite within. To symbolize the Absolute may in some way help the devotee without robbing him of the last spark of human dignity; to lie at the feet of an utterly capricious entity, whose very existence can be disproved by the machinery of human thought, and there to pray for what has not been earned, here is indeed a state of religious affairs which the East may be excused for failing to respect, much less to imitate.

A New Attitude to Circumstances

The field of consciousness may be described as twofold, in concentric circles. First, our circumstance, that which 'stands around', consists of and is seen by consciousness as the physical body, created by human parents, with its good or ill-health, colour, sex and class. Within this lies the emotional body with its developed or undeveloped emotions, its likes and dislikes, hopes and fears; within or 'above' this lies the workaday mind, or rational intellect, with its prejudices, aptitudes and concepts of all kinds; and then? All depends on the height of awareness to which the individual can raise his consciousness. To most of us the intellect is 'I'. But wherever the line be drawn, the perceiving faculty acts and reacts in a wide field of experience which is yet encompassed by the body's skin.

The outward circumstance is wider and more varied still. The home and family life, the day's employment, interests outside the home, all these are circumstance, and from the new point of view are all material for inner growth and nothing more. Said one of the Masters of Zen Buddhism, 'Our Essence of Mind is intrinsically pure, and the reason we are perturbed is because we allow ourselves to be carried away by our circumstances'. And again, 'Our mind should stand aloof from circumstances, and on no account should we allow them to influence the function of our mind'. This does not mean that the ideal is indifference to the world without while locked in a false serenity within. It means that the individual must learn to dominate his circumstance, to decide his reaction, if any, to every happening, from the news in the morning's paper to the loss of his house by fire. He will command himself, and therefore the situation. He will use events for his own high purposes, as an opportunity to do what is 'right', as a chance to learn.

For all of a man's circumstance, his vehicles of awareness and the world around him are his own creation. Whether he likes them or not, he made them, and he cannot fairly complain of what he does not like to any but their creator, that is to say, his own unending processes of thought, desire and action. This being so, how does he learn to make use of circumstance?

P.A.Y.Go

An analogy, not too fanciful, may be drawn from the English method of collecting income tax familiarly known as P.A.Y.E., or pay as you earn. 'Pay as you go' is the Buddhist method, unconscious or deliberate, of coming to terms with karma and its consequences. If a stone be thrown into a pool the disturbance reacts at the point of entry of the stone. In the same way a pendulum when moved swings back as far as the initial impulse. How, when the balance is disturbed, do we restore the equilibrium? As the law demands adjustment, why not make the adjustment here and now? The Roman Catholic practice of confession, penance and absolution, whatever its spiritual value or karmic result, has the merit of swift mental adjustment for wrong done. For the human mind has a craving for balance, and for the restoration of balance disturbed. Indeed, a distinguished judge once spoke of the prisoner's right to punishment, and all who have studied crime and criminals know of the vast relief which many a man exhibits when he knows that retribution, run away from, is now at hand. In brief, when a karmic debt is incurred it is well to pay it, and the wise man tries to pay it on demand.

The philosophic background of P.A.Y.Go is, of course, the unity of life. We are truly members one of another, and the erring member is wise, when a debt is incurred to the Whole, to be swift and generous in payment. First, however, comes confession, to oneself, to the person to whom most lies are usually told. When the error is fully accepted as such let the balance be made. Give, give freely, till it hurts; such is the proper remedy. The Buddhist virtue of Dana, giving, or charity in its widest form, is far more than the distribution of surplus funds. Every injury and complaint, however trivial, should be healed with giving, with measure heaped up, overflowing with goodwill. Give to the man who deserves it, and as much to the man who does not. Give to the thief who swindles you; and again, if he returns for more. Are you the loser? He paid the heavier price. In exchange for what he gained he became a thief. His debt is still unpaid, and what have you lost save a passing possession of the ever-changing physical body? All that is given or lost or stolen from us belongs to the self, the not-Self. Are we not richer without it? Why then do we fail to give away our dearest possession, desire? Or is this our worst liability!

We give of money, and that is the easiest gift. Harder is time to give to those who need our time and thought and interest. The least we can give is gratitude; injuries we must ignore. But the greatest of all gifts is understanding, based, once more, on a growing awareness of life's unity. We live in the ill-lit cages of our limited awareness. We know the desires of 'I', and of their frustration, but we know very little and care not enough for the needs and 'right' desires of others. Yet every relationship that swims into our own karmic ken is a problem for solution, a job of work to be done. Solve the problem, grasp the opportunity; thus is a karmic debt wiped out and the mind ennobled by the deed. Dissolve all links no longer desired by the other side to an agreement. In business, friendship or the sharing of a garden roller, he is a fool who clings. Be generous, then, in loans, which are better as gifts, and in all occasion for understanding. What is Enlightenment but understanding to the nth degree?

The effect of P.A.Y.Go is immediate. It begins to reduce desire. What we find we cannot afford we desire the less. We cease to have karmic credit accounts, and by paying cash we are richer by the payment made. At least we emerge from the incident without making further knots for a future date's unravelling, and freedom from debt is the measure of wealth in heaven. In any event we learn, and a lesson learnt is an account closed, as also an asset gained. Enlightenment is serenity of Mind. Serenity is another name for inward balance, and only when all accounts are balanced can the self which made the entries be allowed to die. The final entry is the death of self, for when the causer has ceased to be there are no more effects. As we pay as we go we hasten the end of self-desiring, and thus remove progressively the ugly, noisy animal which stands between us and the next step on the Way.

Relations with our Fellow Men

Once more the key for the lock of new relationship is the unity of life. Mankind is utterly one, though infinitely various, and the types of men are profoundly different, not only in bodily structure but in basic pattern of mind. The sexes, East and West, the introvert and extravert, these are obvious pairs of opposites, but the functions of the mind are also complementary, as C. G. Jung has proved. All of us, for example, are more developed in feeling or intellect, and the 'inferior function', that which is less developed, is apt to disturb the balance of the whole. The Middle Way is an admirable ideal, but just as man walks upon two legs, from this to that in his progress forward, so, it would seem, we develop alternately the complementary aspects of the mind. It follows, not only that we cannot assume that our neighbour is of the same type as ourselves but that he, being different, must also work out his own salvation with diligence, even though his path be for the time being different from that which is at the moment ours. In the words of an ancient Buddhist saying, 'The ways to the One are as many as the lives of men'.

We contact our neighbour on one or many of several 'planes'. The point of contact may be mainly physical, as in games, or making love, or dressmaking, or war. Or it may be mainly emotional, as in affection or ill-will; or practical-mental, as in business, and common interests, or in government, large or small. Or the link may be higher, on the plane of ideals and abstract reasoning. Here the intuition, the faculty of im-mediate understanding, speaks without words in a common awareness, and the climbers of the mountain begin to see each other as they approach from utterly different points of view. But in every case the relationship is complex, and it is useful to decide what the strength and the range of the interest may be. The best link, that which wears the longest and with most profit to both sides, is the conscious treading of the Path which leads, by a thousand deviations and one right purpose, to supreme Enlightenment. Sometimes a human relationship is clearly 'new'; at times it feels extremely old, as though two colleagues of a life gone by, now possibly of different sex and colour and relative age, were once more met together, to renew, in happy communion, the common way.

One's duty to one's neighbour is, from the Buddhist point of view, to forget the differences of self and self in the greater unity which is Mind-only. In the application of this ideal there is as much variety as in the human mind, for the karmic law, in the long round of successive lives, produces every known relationship. Yet all these human beings are truly brothers, born of one mother, matter, by one father, life. There are older and younger brothers, some to follow and some to lead, but all are members of one family to be served, if need be, at the cost of self and all which the self holds dear. 'The first step', says *The Voice of the Silence*, 'is to live to benefit mankind'. In a way it is also the last. There is no reward for this service; on the contrary, the reaction of the mass to spiritual help is always abuse and persecution. Such is the fate of each reformer, great or small, but the duty of self-sacrifice remains. Only action which benefits the common weal is 'right' action, as only deeds without thought of self are karma-less. Our duty to our neighbour is to serve him with priority over self, and the greatest of gifts is the Dhamma, for by this means he will in time achieve his own Enlightenment. Meanwhile a cup of tea, or a friendly smile, or the willingness to understand may discharge immediate duty. At least we shall, to this extent, have 'ceased to do evil', by hate or cold indifference, and have 'learnt to do good', by the will to help him on the way. So shall we diminish, drop by drop, that 'sea of suffering formed of the tears of men', and in the course of it reduce the self whose death is the birth of Enlightenment.

The practice of these new relationships profoundly affects the deeps of mind and the whole character. All development is now subordinate to the common purpose, greater awareness, brighter light. On the one hand, the sense of a common weal is steadily expanded; on the other, the ultimate importance of the individual, alone the creator of his destiny, is steadily more clearly seen. With the key of Enlightenment the problems of our seemingly unjust and meaningless existence are steadily resolved, and in the place of unending warfare with our circumstance and fellow beings we begin to see the pattern and purpose of that 'power which moves to righteousness', which is the One as it moves in the Many, the awareness in each of us that one day every blade of grass will enter into Enlightenment.

18

Buddhist Values and the Buddhist Way

The term 'Buddhism', used since its creation for the vast body of doctrine, ceremony, culture, and art built up about the teaching of Gautama Siddhartha, the Buddha, has two distinct sources, one esoteric and the other exoteric. According to the esoteric tradition, for those who wrote the 'Mahatma Letters' to A. P. Sinnett and to their pupil, H. P. Blavatsky, there has ever been 'the accumulated wisdom of the ages, tested and verified by generations of seers', and this Wisdom is the tree from which all the known and now forgotten religions emerged as branches large and small. The Wisdom has its guardians, those who in their spiritual evolution became masters of the laws of life, of the powers latent in man, and hence the natural guardians of the knowledge by which that status was attained. The Master of these Masters, 'the patron of all the adepts', 'the reformer and codifier of the occult system', as he was called, was the Buddha, the latest of his line, 'the greatest and the holiest man that ever lived'. His supreme Enlightenment, so great that 'his spirit could at one and the same time rove interstellar spaces in full consciousness, and continue at will on earth in his original and undivided body', was the indescribable experience which his teaching was an attempt to describe. But it is this teaching, only partly understood and imperfectly remembered until, much 'edited', it was written down five hundred years later, which is exoteric

Buddhism—still, however, according to those same Masters, the nearest to the esoteric Wisdom of any faith extant.

The life of Gautama the Buddha is itself the prototype of Buddhist values. When a young princeling, beautiful, brilliant, accomplished in the arts of peace and war and heir to his father's kingdom, leaves his wife and new-born child and retires to the forest as a mendicant monk in rags, there must be a powerful stimulus to such a change. But for him the will to *know*, to find out for himself and all mankind the cause of that inevitable suffering which lay behind this ideal happiness, was paramount, even to his decision to forego the supreme reward—Nirvana—for the knowledge gained was the prototype of spiritual compassion utterly applied. And the Buddha was a man, no God, with the declared consequence that, what one did, all other men in time can do.

What did he teach? If this is difficult at times to say with certainty, at least we know, according to the Pali canon, precisely what he did not teach and even refused to discuss. When Potthapada, the wandering mendicant, wanted to know whether the world is eternal, whether the soul is the same as the body, and so on, and when another mendicant, Vacchagotta, wanted to know whether or not there is a Self, the answer was definite: the Buddha refused to say. And he gave as his reason that such discussion, being impossible of purely intellectual answer and having no relation to what should be man's perpetual and whole-time occupation, was sheer waste of time. Yet it must be assumed that this tremendous mind completely knew the answers, in that his range of consciousness was immeasurable. He chose, then, not to expound the outline of the esoteric doctrine which we have in *The Secret Doctrine* by H. P. Blavatsky, but to concentrate his disciples' minds—on what? 'This do I teach, O Bhikkhus, suffering and the end of suffering.' Just as the ocean and every drop of it has the same savour—salt —so all things living share the selfsame suffering. This was the primal, direct experience which life revealed to him, and he left his father's palace with the unshakable resolve to find its cause.

He found it, under the moon of Wesak under the Bodhi tree, whose descendant stands in Buddha Gaya to this day. And his message to mankind is a long description of the Way by which he made this shaking, mind-releasing discovery. 'The Tathagata is one who shows the Way.' Or, in the words of the *Dhamma-pada*, 'Even Buddhas do but show the Way'. Such is the value of the Way, to be trodden by every man to his own and the world's salvation, that all else in the teaching, as all else in daily life, is made subordinate. This is the test of teaching wheresoever learned, that it does or does not assist that journey to the heart's release from suffering by the ending of its cause, desire. If the Theravada, 'the teaching of the Elders', is a magnificent moral philosophy it is, according to the members of that school, because it never moves from the Middle Way of the Eightfold Path prescribed.

The value of the Way itself is as unique in the field of religion as the limits set by the Buddha on the ambit of his message to mankind. There is no dogma; all is open to enquiry and analysis, as open as any scientific thesis offered to the world today. Nay, more; this is the only religion known to man in which the Founder himself forbids his followers to accept a single word of doctrine merely because he himself proclaims it. As he said in his famous advice to the Kalamas, 'Do not be misled by report or tradition or hearsay. Nor by logic and inference and reasons, *nor because the recluse* (who holds it) *is your teacher.* But when you find that doctrines (when applied) conduce to dispassion, to decrease of worldly gain, to contentment and delight in good' (and thus to the heart's release from suffering) 'then adopt them.' In other words, take each and every teaching as a working hypothesis, test it, and if it works then make it yours. Could anything be further from the chains of dogma?

But the Path is of course within, as indeed all spiritual life is wholly within. 'Work out your own salvation with diligence', said the Buddha with his dying words. No word here of a Saviour, for in Buddhism there is none. Each man treads the Path by his own efforts on his own two feet, and though he walks with all mankind beside him, the journey from here and now to full Enlightenment is his to begin and his to end. None can do more than aid him as a guide; none shall stand between him and the glory earned.

But travel has its rules, and the law of karma, the cosmic law of universal harmony, reigns supreme. 'I will teach you

Dhamma,' said the Buddha. 'If this is, that comes to be; from the arising of this, that arises; if this is not, that does not come to be; from the ceasing of this, that ceases.' This is surely one of the most profound statements of universal truth ever pronounced. The doctrine of karma was old when Buddhism was born, but this tremendous, all-embracing statement of it opened a new field of spiritual understanding. Nor can it be lightly held. 'Wonderful, Lord!' said the Buddha's favourite disciple, Ananda, 'How deep is this causal law, yet do I regard it as plain to understand!' 'Say not so, Ananda,' the Buddha replied. 'It is by not knowing, by not understanding, by not penetrating this doctrine that this world of men has become entangled like a ball of twine, and unable to pass beyond suffering and the ceaseless round of rebirth.'

Thus man is thrown back on his own resources to the consequences, whether he views them as good or ill, of his own thought and will and deed. By right action he earns merit; by wrong, demerit and its multiple consequence, but whether he views the results as good or ill he may not escape them. 'Not in the sky, not in the sea, not in the cave in the mountains,' says the *Dhammapada*, 'can a man escape from his evil deeds', and the same applies to his good deeds which, if done with the least thought of self, will also bring him back to birth to receive the due reward. Even his aggression, the wrongly focused will, must be in the end digested and inturned. 'Though a man should conquer a thousand times a thousand men in battle, he who conquers himself is the greatest warrior.' This living law accepted, even as hypothesis, a man can be truly master of his destiny, in this life and in lives to come. For the doctrine of rebirth is twin to karma, and a necessary corollary. True, each unit of life, large or small, is changing so rapidly that it is in a sense reborn each second of time, but the larger cycle is no less true. Even as we sleep at the end of the day and wake refreshed to begin where we left off on the night before, so in each new life of the inward self a wide new field appears in which, with fresh experiences, new lessons may be learned. Here are new values for the West indeed, to drop the teaching of a single life with an everlasting Judgment at the end, for belief in a period of experience on earth, then the purgatory of desire unsatisfied and the heaven of aspirations seemingly fulfilled, and rebirth for fresh experience.

Is a picture of Buddhist values beginning to emerge? No God, no Saviour, but every man a busy gardener removing weeds and cultivating virtues; or, to change the simile, concerned with the purification and then the expansion of his own consciousness until, like that of the Buddha, it is commensurate with the universe. None can hurry the pilgrim on this Way; none can prevent his reaching the goal. The task in hand has supreme value—not worship, nor ceremony, but the next thing to be done, and whenever possible the next thing to be done in the service of his neighbour.

While treading this daily, hourly Way, he is steadily expanding the mind, not his own mind but his approach to the Universal Mind of THAT, which the Buddha called the 'Unborn, Not-become, Not-made'. The entrance to the Way is Right Views, intellectual understanding of the basic laws of the universe; then comes Morality in its widest sense of character-building; then, and of paramount value, the systematic expansion of consciousness which in time becomes

> A heart untouched by worldly things, a heart
>   that is not swayed
> By sorrow, a heart passionless, secure;
> That is the greatest blessing.

But this is not the end. Even the utmost intensity of thought will never *know*; it will but know *about*. Only the intuition, the built-in faculty of direct awareness, knows, and it matters not how this awareness is achieved. Nirvana is not a negative but the supreme Affirmation dimly described by Thoreau: 'I know that the enterprise is worthy. I know that things work well. I have heard no bad news.'

All Buddhist values merge upon this goal with its savour of release from suffering, from the untrue sense of separation, from the illusion of things unlit by the glow of Enlightenment.

As such Nirvana has no value for it is that which gives value to all else. It is human awareness of the 'Unborn, Not-created, Not-formed', the Absolute. Yet it is, and must be found, here—

not in heaven; now, not only after death; and in doing this—the next thing to be done. 'In this six foot body,' said the Buddha, 'is to be found the world, and the origin of the world, and the Way that leads to the ceasing of it.'

In practice, this is where the Way divides into complementary aspects of itself. The ideal man of the older, Therevada School, is that of the Arhat, who concentrates on purging his mind of defilements and expanding it immeasurably. His doctrines and practices are largely of the head. The later Mahayana School was complementary, compassion ranking with wisdom as its other half, the heart at least as valuable as the head, and the ideal man the Bodhisattva who, caring nothing for his own salvation, is vowed to dedicate his being and his every act to the salvation of each form of life, 'until the last blade of grass shall enter into Buddhahood'. These aspects are reflections of the relative types of the human mind, but in the end there is a true choice to be made. At least, so says *The Voice of the Silence,* and its words are clear. In *The Secret Doctrine* we have an exposition of the doctrine; in the section on Probation and Chelaship in *The Mahatma Letters* to A. P. Sinnett we have an account of what the would-be pupil must by himself achieve before he is worthy of true discipleship. And then? We must begin to choose. 'Compassion speaks and saith: "Can there be bliss when all that lives must suffer? Shalt thou be saved and hear the whole world cry?"' Here is personal value accorded to the two paths which open. True, none can help mankind until he trains himself to such a service, and self-salvation interpreted exclusively is incompatible with the end of a sense of self. But the choice as outlined in the *Voice* applies to all mankind of whatever temperament. Either one's ultimate purpose, which here means sense of values, is to serve the whole or it is but to serve the part, and the part at best but a glorified version of oneself. The former is the way of the All-Compassionate One, the Buddha. With the latter we are not concerned. The supreme value of all religion is to serve the high purposes of THAT which, being manifest, is all that we are and know. The rest are lesser values to be outgrown in pain and suffering.

Rootless Thought

We've lost our first beginnings, the great power
Of wonder and amaze. Intemperate thought,
Boastful of each precision concept wrought
Must wither, as a rootless, severed flower
When ravished and bereft of nourishment.
The conscious heart, a lotus on the pool
Of unawareness, with compassion full
And void of difference, is well content
To feel the sun of life, the wind of pain
In all things visible, softly to kneel
Before the truth in myth enshrined, to heal
The wounded soul with symbol, and retain
The motherhood of earth.
                              Proud thought alone
Is barren, breeds but thought again, and dies
Before the Namelessness, whose naked eyes
See utterly the faceless Known-Unknown.
Only the heart, the spirit's lantern, knows
The root and holiness of thought awing,
The splendour of the spirit's flowering,
The dawn wind and the summer rose.

Release anew the springs of life; drink deep
The wisdom that we do not know; arrest
The flight of self in gilded thought expressed,
And in the wholeness of becoming reap
The guerdon of humility. Then mind
And heart, the intellect a proven tool
In service of the One Unknowable,
Shall climb beyond and seek and haply find.

19

The Many and the One

The Buddha discouraged in his Teaching all speculation—and it is but speculation for the unenlightened—on the nature of the First Cause, or the Final Effect. It was not that he did not understand the process whereby the Unmanifest came into manifestation. On the contrary; 'The arising of the world, Brethren, hath been fully understood by the Tathagata. . . . The ceasing of the world, Brethren, hath been fully understood by the Tathagata. . . . The Way going to the ceasing of the world hath been fully understood by the Tathagata.' . . . Indeed, he could remember it. 'I, Brethren, when I so desire it, can call to mind my previous states of birth . . . up to a hundred thousand births; the various destructions of aeons, the various renewals of aeons. . . . ' He could even describe the chronology of these cosmic events. 'I myself can bear witness to having reaped for many a long day the profit of good works. . . . For seven years I practised kindly thought, and (as a result) I came back not into this world for seven aeons of the involution and evolution of the world.' And he goes on to describe his state of consciousness at the time. It was not, then, because of lack of knowledge that he would not speak of these things, but because he saw, with his unrivalled vision into the working of men's minds, that speculation on these subjects was not only useless but an actual hindrance on the Way. And why? Because it tended to distract the mind from the constant effort needed to achieve its own release from the fetters of Samsara.

But the human mind, while claiming to desire the truth, is

ever prone to sit and discuss what it may be, in preference to making the actual effort to find out. The All-Enlightened One had scarcely vanished from the eyes of men before the speculative Indian mind was hard at work to acquire the knowledge which the Blessed One had said they did not at the moment need. In the course of centuries some measure of the Ancient Wisdom, that ever-growing store of knowledge, tested and verified by generations of those who achieve liberation, was rediscovered and described by some of the mighty thinkers who wore the Robe. They studied and won to awareness, and wrote what may be written of what they found. And so, as the Western mind is naturally curious about ultimates, it may be useful to give some background, however nebulous, to the foreground of the Buddhist Way.

The subject of the One and the Many may be approached from the Many or from the One. The Buddhist approaches it first from the Many, for that is the scientific and the Buddhist method of approaching Truth. We know the Many through the senses, the emotions and the mind, and we know, as the Buddha taught us to confirm for ourselves, that it is, in all its parts, *anicca,* changing, *dukkha,* inseparable from suffering, and *anatta,* lacking any immortal part or soul which is the exclusive property of that part. Such being the Many we naturally, and with a powerful inner urge, seek for that which lacks these attributes. And the Buddha agreed that the search would not be vain. To quote once again, 'There is, O Bhikkhus, an Unborn, a Not-become, a Not-made, a Not-compounded. (For) if there were not, O Bhikkus, an Unborn, a Not-become, a Not-made, a Not-compounded, there could be no escape from the born, become, made, compounded . . . ' The existence, then, of the Unborn, the noumenon of all phenomena, is at least a logical hypothesis, and it is interesting to note the intensity with which men seek it, though they seek it in many ways. Indeed the Buddhist saying, 'The ways to the One are as many as the lives of men', is consonant to the Buddha's dying injunction to each and every man : 'Work out your own salvation with diligence'.

Mankind may be divided into those who seek the Ultimate and those who drift as dead leaves on the river of time. It is for the former, the comparatively few, that all the Sages strive to record their wisdom, by whatever name that Wisdom may be known. On the physical plane the scientist analyses matter. Finding no unity in the least unit which he can, with all his apparatus, sense or see, he splits the atom into a larger Many, and risks the destruction of all humanity in his zeal. And what does he find? The end of matter; no substance that is not in motion, motion which is the mode, the means, the expression of Life. Those who work through the emotions, using the technique of Bhakti Yoga, or the arts, or the many forms of religion, likewise seek the Imperishable within the forms that perish, the Ideal of beauty or love as their way may be. On the mental plane, the approach is as various as the colours of the spectrum, colours that are the unreal garments of primordial light. The philosopher who seeks Reality; the metaphysician who builds his tower of concept till its summit is illumined with the Light he seeks; the mystic who, while using thought and feeling, develops the faculty of *buddhi*, the intuition, to *know* where he did but know about; the psychologist who, working within his own confessed limitations, yet finds in his patients' minds the healing symbols which heal because they are symbols of a basic unity; the doctor whose task is health, which is wholeness; the moralist who strives to base all action on laws which are moral because they reflect a primordial and unsevered Will, all these are pilgrims seeking the Way and a Guide upon it.

> We are the pilgrims, Master; we shall go
>   Always a little further; it may be
> Beyond that last blue mountain barred with snow
>   Across that angry or that glimmering sea,
> White on a throne or guarded in a cave,
>   There lives a prophet who can understand
> Why men were born.[1]

'Always a little further.' Yet, however far the distance the pilgrims move towards one or other of the two great pillars on which the Dhamma rests, Prajna, supreme Wisdom, and Karuna, supreme Compassion, are utterly and gloriously One. Indeed, the assault on the Everest of Truth will prove the falsity of all the pairs of opposites, and the Buddhist knows that he

[1] From *Hassan*, Act V. Elroy Flecker.

must accept the experience that each is equally true, that black is white and night is day, not in spite of their mutual exclusion but because of it.

Meanwhile the pilgrims seek the One as a living experience. They find the intellect to be a guide upon the Way so far and then no further. The thought-machine knows this and that, and more and more about each part of it. It does not and it cannot know. For this some higher faculty than thought is needed, and it lies in the intuition, the human faculty of direct awareness. It is, as it were, a lamp, or large or small, at the summit of the purely human faculties, through which the Light of the One irradiates each aspect of the Many. Without its development, the intellect remains the scholar; with it, the pilgrim enters the stage of One-awareness. As a Buddhist he will, if of the Theravada School, first analyze each aspect of the Many, and learn to observe with steady gaze — 'mindful and self-possessed' — each single thing as it is. Yet sooner or later he will, from this cold, analytic intellectual march, enlarge his vision with the working concepts of the Mahayana School. Here, as already described, the doctrine of *anatta* is enlarged to that of the primordial Void; the nature of each and every thing is seen in its final suchness or *tathata*; and consciousness is known at a higher level, that of the Unconscious of Mu-shin, 'No-mind', a state beyond thinking, of Mind-only, a wakened reunion with that Mind of which each human mind is a reflex, each part the conscious part of the supernal Whole.

At such a level of awareness, however gained, the pilgrim will rediscover for himself that accumulated wisdom of the ages which speaks of the coming into being of the Universe with the voice of those who know. There will then be time enough to study the Many and the One from the viewpoint of the One. The Wisdom is well expressed in the Proem to The Secret *Doctrine*, as written by H. P. Blavatsky, but it is to be found, truncated and distorted, in all the great religions and philosophies of mankind.

And at the end? The greatest discovery of all. All other religions and philosophies display the threefold parts of a journey, the beginning, the journey, and the end, and always the journey is from the Unreal to the Real, from the world as we know it to a heavenly and entirely other Ideal. Buddhism alone knows no escapism, no attempt to remove from the here and now to a hypothetical then. For when the Many is known in all its parts and principles, and the One achieved as a known experience by this road or that, the final fact of Life is itself revealed, that the One and the Many are themselves correlatives; Nirvana *is* in fact Samsara, the beginning and the end of the journey are motion without movement, the Many and the One are a two-fold unity.

> The One is none other than the All, the All
>   none other than the one.
> Take your stand on this, and the rest will follow
>   of its own accord.[1]

Only, then, when the final pairs of opposites are transcended, and the ultimate Two made One, is the Goal in sight. In the words of Dr Evans-Wentz, 'Life, being a fabric of correlative, independent, interacting dualities, cannot be understood without knowing both aspects of the dualities; and the Great Liberation is consequent upon attaining that state of transcendence wherein all dualities become undifferentiated Wisdom'. And again, 'Complete realization of the essential and undifferentiated oneness of the Samsara and Nirvana which, according to the Mahayana, are the Ultimate Duality, leads to that Deliverance of the Mind taught by the Enlightened One as being the aim and end of the Dharma.'[2]

Even this is not the end. For, as pertinently asked by the Zen Master, 'If all returns to the One, to what does the One return?' To this there is only one answer, and it explains so well why the All-Enlightened One refused to indulge the demand for news of the Ultimates—'Walk on!'

[1] From the poem, 'On Trust in the Heart' by Seng-ts'an trans. Takakusu. Taken from *Buddhist Texts*. Edward Conze, p. 298.
[2] *The Tibetan Book of the Great Liberation*, pp. 37 et seq.

20

The Field of Mahayana Buddhism

The Theravada is the oldest extant school of Buddhism. If such was the Buddha's teaching it seems to have been deliberately limited in scope, yet it includes the fundamental principles which I have called Basic Buddhism. These include the Three Signs of Being, the Four Noble Truths, the Noble Eightfold Path, Karma and Rebirth, the nature of Nirvana, the essential tolerance of Buddhism and its complete absence of dogma or authority, human or divine.

Soon after the Buddha's death, however, there arose in India what its members called a Mahayana, a larger vehicle (of salvation) as distinct from what some of them called the Hinayana, smaller vehicle, the group of sects of which the eighteenth survives today as the Theravada. Quite soon the new range of teaching became large and varied in relation to the earlier school, and it is still growing today. When, for example, I compiled *The Wisdom of Buddhism*, an anthology of Buddhist Scriptures, I did not hesitate, in the absence of any ancient writing covering the subject, to include a description by the late Dr D. T. Suzuki of the doctrine of Jijimuge, 'the unimpeded interdiffusion of all particulars', which is the essence of the Kegon School of Japan.

The Mahayana School was born in North-East India at one of the Councils held after the Master's death by his followers. Just why it was born is still debated; my own view is that it was inevitable, being complementary in terms of doctrine and the mind's experience. Although the Theravada was complete in itself as a moral philosophy, the Indian mind was not content with it. The Buddha, according to the Theravada, limited his teaching on the ground that argument on 'ultimates' clouds the real purpose of the practising Buddhist, which is to kill out the 'three fires' of hatred, lust and illusion aflame within his mind, and to expand his consciousness by strenuous training to the achievement of Nirvana. The Indian mind refused to rest there. It is true that when the Buddhist Emperor Asoka sent his son to Ceylon to 'proclaim the Dhamma' he took with him Theravada Buddhism, but it was the Mahayana which went North to Tibet and Mongolia, East along the old silk road to China, Korea and Japan.

The Buddhism of the Southern School is not a religion. It has no God, no prayer to that God, and no priests to intercede with that God for the benefit of an immortal soul. Its ideal was the Arhat, the worthy one who by enormous effort developed his mind to complete enlightenment. Being safely rooted in Ceylon, this school survived the Mahommedan conquest of India in which the monasteries of then surviving Buddhism were ruthlessly destroyed. But it did no more than survive. Save for Buddhaghosa of the fourth century A.D. it produced no scholar of note or original thinker, but it did preserve intact, save for the monkish editing of the early texts, the basic teachings of that school.

Meanwhile, at a date difficult to fix, there occurred in the Buddha's homeland what can only be described as an explosion, an explosion of thought, the 'fall-out' of which carried the doctrines of the earlier school into the field of metaphysics, mysticism and even religion in its popular form. The mind behind it was Nagarjuna, who founded a body of literature, to grow in succeeding centuries to enormous bulk, which concerned itself with Prajna-paramita, 'the Wisdom which has gone beyond', which Dr Edward Conze, the leading scholar on the subject, has called the Perfection of Wisdom. It certainly rose beyond thought, beyond the Oneness beloved of mystics, for, as a Ch'an master of old enquired, 'When all things return to the One to what does the One return? And the only answer is 'Non-duality', that which is neither one nor two. This Non-duality was called the Void, *sunya*, a Voidness of all things, all concepts, predicates or ideas, of all that can be described or taught or believed, of all that can be understood. Hence a famous master's remark on being asked about Buddhism, 'I do not understand Buddhism'. Even as a concept, this Void, so empty that it is empty of emptiness, is surely the ultimate height of human thought; thought can go no further. And in actual experience it takes one to the very threshold of the 'Unborn, Unoriginated, Unformed' as the Buddha called the Absolute. It is the Everest of human thought.

It speaks from the actual experience of Non-duality. It is therefore thought illumined by the intuition, illumined thinking, and Dr Suzuki called it indeed 'a system of intuitions'. True understanding of it requires a leap from the bonds of logic to 'the other shore', and any attempt to understand it without some measure of this experience creates but more confusion. At the very least, those who would understand the Mahayana must learn to discard conceptual argument.

For in a sense there is nothing to be understood. The whole literature of the Prajnaparamita is but a thousand statements that nothing *is*—'there is *no thing*'! There is but THAT which lies beyond all things, an absolute Void of things which nevertheless is at the same time absolutely full! Only by understanding this can one understand the heart of the Mahayana. For the manifold schools and subdivisions are, for all their external differences, so many ways of becoming aware of that which lies 'beyond'.

From the hundred foot pole, as the Chinese say, at the top of which is the height of thought, we must take the existential leap to direct awareness, and this super-thinking is, in particular, the springboard of the Chinese 'Ch'an' which became in Japan 'Zen' Buddhism. It is the state of mind of the master who can consciously achieve some measure of this awareness and, to the extent that words can speak, speak from it. And the literature, deeply studied, rouses the intuition to the direct experience from which the words were given forth. This is why Dr Suzuki says that 'Buddhism is personal experience and not impersonal philosophy'. In the end the ideal is 'to let the mind alight nowhere', meaning that although in a relative world a multitude of concepts—and words are concepts frozen into sound—must be used, in the end *all* concepts must be abandoned.

Much follows from this basic understanding of the Prajna-paramita philosophy. We understand now why it is said that Nirvana *is* Samsara, that the world about us, the world of becoming, *is* the world of Nirvana, which is the absolute. There cannot be two things, the relative and the absolute; they are one. On the relative plane we see them as duality; on the higher plane we see the two as one. There is only, to use another term of the Mahayana, the *tathata* or 'suchness' of each thing, each being, that which makes it what it is; and this is the 'suchness' of all other things and beings. And that 'suchness' is Void. The only reality at the heart of any thing, whether it be the atom or the universe, is that which is not there, that which is beyond the limitations of form; the Formless. And that is why all beings and all things alive are one, and there is nothing that is not alive. While moving, we must know the Immovable. Life is movement; the Immovable is that from which life came. We must learn to live life as life lives itself, as an expression of the 'Unborn, Unoriginated, Unformed'. We must learn to live totally, sufficiently, here and now; within ourselves and not 'projecting' or trying to escape. For nowhere shall we escape from our selves, wherever we may take our selves, and whatever we do. Inside each self is found Nirvana and the Void; and at the heart of all that we can conceive is the Inconceivable.

This supernal field of literature is known to us best through two scriptures, the Diamond Sutra and the Heart Sutra. Both are recited daily throughout Tibet, China and Japan and there are many translations available. Yet even these two are but saying again and again, 'Form is emptiness and the very emptiness is form. Form does not differ from emptiness; emptiness does not differ from form.' There is no wisdom to be found in words or forms. Wisdom lies beyond and the beyond lies within.

The relationship between the Theravada and the Mahayana is now more easy to understand. From the limited though splendid moral-philosophy of the earlier school there is at once an expansion and a lift; an expansion sideways and a lift to a higher level of consciousness in intuitive awareness. The dual process is but dual in analogy; the growth is in all dimensions all the time.

The expansion can be described to some extent in terms of doctrine. Perhaps there are four which, common to the sects of the Mahayana, are to be distinguished from the Pali canon of the southern school. Yet all are developments from or complementary to this Basic Buddhism, and the analogy of spokes of a wheel expanding from the hub to a far circumference is sound.

First, there is the fact that the Buddha moved through the centuries from the historic figure of Gautama Siddhartha, a princeling of India, to 'the Buddha within', the Buddha Nature, which ever was and will be, beyond time, beyond space, immovable. Within, without; everything about us only relatively exists, and absolutely does not exist at all. This is the doctrine of *anicca/anatta* of the Theravada taken to its nth degree, and raised to the experience of *sunyata*, the Void. It is not merely that there is no permanent, abiding self in man; there is no permanent abiding self in anything; there are no things in which it could abide. There is no thing, only no-thing-ness, which if we like to indulge in capitals, is the Absolute, the Light, and the Joy which makes all life worth living. I *am* Buddha, because all things are Buddha, because all things are expressions of that Lifeforce which is an expression of THAT which is Buddhahood, the Buddha within. There is therefore no question of acquiring anything or indeed of learning anything. I have but to become what I am, to know what in truth I am. And I can do this independently of history. The Buddhist schools are not agreed on the actual date of the Buddha's birth and death, and they are unconcerned with their uncertainty. It does not matter when the Buddha lived; in a sense it does not matter to the Buddhist that he lived as alleged at all. For in every being is the Buddha nature, the Essence of Mind, the Light of the Unborn, and every man can find it. Nevertheless, the human being who, after innumerable lives of effort, expanded his consciousness to the limits of the universe, is one we may with reverence adore in gratitude. For he it was who found the Way to this awareness and proclaimed it to all mankind.

We now see what is meant by the lift. *Anicca/anatta*, the statement that all is change and that no thing has any permanent, separate self, is lifted to the level of *sunyata*, that all things whatsoever are utterly Void. In the same way *metta*, loving-kindness, a most excellent virtue, is raised to the level of Karuna, impersonal compassion, not merely as a heightened form of love but as 'the Law of Laws, eternal Harmony'. In the same way Prajna, supernal Wisdom, is utterly beyond the reach of intellectual knowledge, and Karuna is its expression in a thousand 'skilful means'. Such Wisdom/Compassion is not of the daily mind. We must think until thought is exhausted, and with a will which knows no pause break through the 'thought-barrier' to a heart awakened to compassion for all living things. And the wakening follows the death of the sense of separation in which and in which alone the ego-sense had lived.

The second doctrine which developed in the Mahayana is the complementary, ideal figure of the Bodhisattva, he whose essence, *sattva*, is *bodhi*, Wisdom, in the sense above described. Whereas the Arhat is concerned with his own deliverance the Bodhisattva is concerned in the first place with every deed of help which will bring salvation to all mankind. His Vow is paramount: 'Let others gain Enlightenment; I shall not enter Nirvana until the last blade of grass has entered Buddahood.' For him, in the words of *The Voice of the Silence*, 'the first step is to live to benefit mankind'.

But these ideals are clearly complementary; neither is better than the other. In the end both are discarded, both retained. Diagrammatically, the one moves up to Enlightenment — for himself. As he rightly says, 'How can I purify any other mind than my own?' The other, working outwardly, announces, 'I am not concerned with the Enlightenment of me; I am too busy to focus my attention upon me. I live but to serve mankind.' But even as both are exaggerated aspects of a common whole, so each can be abused. It is easy for the would-be Arhat to say to the would-be Bodhisattva that it is much easier and more pleasant to tell other people what to do than to remove from one's own mind what Sir Edwin Arnold called 'one fond offence'. The reply might be, 'You Arhats are so busy trying to save your souls that you have no time for the woes of humanity. That is selfishness.' To which the Arhat might reply, 'This is not selfishness. I could not tread the path to Enlightenment so long as I retained a sense of self!' And so the argument goes on, quite uselessly. For the two ideals are as complementary as the head and heart, wisdom and compassion, the part and the whole. The student-practiser, new to Buddhism, may choose which he will, according to his 'conditioning'. In the end he will use and discard both.

The next of the four developments of the Mahayana may be called a sense of lift. Just as 'no immortal soul' is raised to the ultimate concept of the Void; just as *metta*, love, moves up to compassion as a universal force, so the Right Action of the Noble Eightfold Path becomes non-action, the *wei-wu-wei* of Taoism and the Bhagavad Gita. For at its best, right action is no-action, where there is no self left to act. Again, right purpose is raised to no-purpose, purposelessness, wherein each thing to be done is done because it is the next thing to be done, with no 'why'! Pansil, the negatively expressed Five Precepts of the Theravada, becomes the positively expressed six *Paramitas* or virtues of the Bodhisattva, and great stress is laid on them. Here is the answer to critics of Buddhism who complain that it is unconcerned with what is now called social service. But, as Dr Suzuki once wrote, 'Practising the Paramitas means the assertion of humanity as a social being, the basic idea being that individuals cannot be perfect until society itself is made perfect. This will naturally mean that an individual becomes perfect when he loses his individuality in the All to which he belongs.' From a path to Nirvana for the individual the Buddha's Middle Way becomes a way for living life as an undivided whole. Samsara is *seen* to be Nirvana, the distinct yet interdiffused two sides of a penny. It follows that to speak of escape from Samsara is folly; there can be no escape save to perceive that in this vale of woe, as man has made it, we may achieve a bliss unutterable.

A fourth difference is the status of the monk. Whereas in the earliest school the bhikkhu is regarded as the true Buddhist, to whom the Buddha gave his teachings or most of them, and but for whom the Dharma would soon cease to exist, in the Mahayana the layman can attain salvation as such. The man, or woman, who enters the monastic life is respected for having given up the sweets of sensuous existence in exchange for unlimited time in which to meditate or by other means to attain the mind's enlightenment, but that is all. The layman who is 'mindful' through the day of the true purpose of life, to slay the self as the cause of suffering, is also and equally upon the Way. Indeed in the Zen school of Japan there are several Roshis, masters, who are laymen, and the two major schools concerned with the Prajnaparamita teaching were schools of thought open to all rather than sects of Buddhism.

This spiritual ferment went on for nearly a thousand years. By A.D. 500 Buddhism had become the largest field of thought extant, and it still is. To the moral philosophy of the Theravada, with its own elaborate psychology and school of meditation, was added a range of philosophy perhaps the highest known, schools of metaphysics and mysticism second to none, and in particular what may be called the mystical metaphysics of the two schools formed within the field of 'the Wisdom which has gone beyond'. One of these, founded by Nagarjuna, the greatest mind of Buddhism, was known as the Madhyamika, the Middle Way between Yes and No, between every conceivable pair of opposites to that which lies behind and beyond both. And the later school of Mind-only, the Yogachara teaching of subjective idealism founded by Vasubandhu and his brother Asanga, applied this metaphysical teaching to the field of psychology with its doctrine of Alaya-Vijnana or 'store-consciousness', which has affinities with the unconscious of Western psychology.

There are many other schools, or traditions as the Tibetans call them, in the Mahayana. The Pure Land, the largest in modern Japan, had its roots in India, and as developed by Shinran Shonen in Japan approached most nearly to the Western concept of religion. This worship of Amida Buddha is on the face of it alien to the main stream of Buddhist development, and it is sad that Dr D. T. Suzuki had no time to make clear to the West what he taught to some of us, that, properly understood, it is but a complement to Zen.

Ch'an Buddhism which, when it arrived in Japan became known as Zen, was born in China in the sixth century as a revolt from the wordy metaphysics of Indian Buddhism. Dynamic, direct, eschewing the aids of doctrine and the intellect, its followers strive mightily for the breakthrough to the beyond of thought. The only major school of Buddhism to have originated outside India, it aims at applying in each human mind the intuitive truths of the Prajnaparamita, and its success is shown among other ways, in the high culture and art which it produced in China and Japan.

The Kegon School of Japan is based on the Avatamsaka Sutra and circles about the intensely difficult doctrine of *Jijimuge*, 'the unimpeded interdiffusion of all particulars', while the Tendai School, a synthesis of many views, is based on the Saddharma-pundarika Sutra, the Lotus of the Good Law. The Shingon School of Japan arrived from China, whither it was taken by travellers from India who had knowledge of the Tantra of Bengal which became so popular, in a slightly altered form, in Tibet.

The last school of the Mahayana which there is space to mention is that of Tibet. Until recently our knowledge of it was incomplete and inaccurate, and it is a happy outcome of the horror of the Chinese invasion of Tibet that a number of high-ranking Lamas escaped to India and now, learning English, are able to release a greater knowledge, not only of the doctrine of the major Buddhist schools of Tibet, but something of its practice of meditation and religious art.

Then Buddhism came West, just sixty years ago. It travelled by schools, as always, not as 'Buddhism'. The Theravada was first in the field; then Zen in the works of Dr D. T. Suzuki, and for a while the Buddhism of England was like the wings of a bird which had no body. For students tended to divide between the Pali canon and the intuitive glories of such works as the Platform Sutra of Hui-neng and the teachings of Huang Po. Few had the mental energy to tackle the Prajnaparamita literature in its many volumes, but Dr Edward Conze, in his *Selected Sayings from the Perfection of Wisdom*, has made its essence available to all.

Will there be a Western Buddhism, in which the two schools will be in some way fused? Why not? After all, the same spiritual impulse, the same basic teaching, flowed into many countries and in each was modified by the people to whom it came. There were already several 'Buddhisms', in Ceylon, Tibet and Japan; nevertheless they are aspects, expressions, of the same Buddhism. Why should the West not form its own, not deliberately but as it happens in the course of time? It well may choose what is native to its genius, what is needed to fill the vacuum of its religious life. In the years to come it may produce its own body of teaching, its own formulae, ritual and method of applying the same unchanging principles.

Such is a rapid survey of an enormous field, wider than the Theravada in its range of thought, in the use and training of the intuition, in including the heart as coeval with the mind. In a sense the field is full, for it seems to include most aspects of the mind's endeavour. If the Theravada caters for the Puritan element in the English mind, the divers schools of the Mahayana satisfy the devotional ideal, and the need of a mystical-intuitive approach to the beyond of sense, which appears at times as non-sense. Here is food for the extrovert and the introvert, the monk and the man of the world, the love of tradition and the claims of the new; all these are working in intimate relationship, and all work from the centre, the heart of Buddhism which is and ever must be the Buddha's Enlightenment. In this great field the student may wander at will, but none will understand the nobility of that vast and glorious whole we know as Buddhism unless he faces and includes what I have called the explosion, the swift and almost sudden lifting of what was an intellectual, rational way of life into a field which has never been rivalled by the human mind, nor exceeded in its range and splendour.

21

The Buddhist Conception of Immanence

From an Address to the World Congress
of Faith in October, 1964

It is basic to all schools of Buddhism that there is no distinction between transcendence and immanence. These are two names for two aspects of the same thing. You can give a name to one side of a penny and another name to the other but they remain aspects of the same thing and have no meaning apart from each other. In the words of a famous Zen master, 'All distinctions are falsely imagined'. Every pair of opposites is illusion as such. All distinction, all pairs of opposites, all man-created differences, are 'falsely imagined'. Immanence is what it is by virtue of the truth of transcendence. Transcendence is what it is by the virtue of immanence and not otherwise.

The most profound statement made in Eastern thought is that 'Nirvana IS Samsara'. The supreme state conceivable for the human mind is only referable to 'here, now and this'. There is no place where one may go and find Nirvana. There is no state of consciousness to be achieved and to be called Nirvana. Nirvana, to the extent that it has any meaning at all, is here, now and this. The journey is a journey from here to there, but there is no distinction between them. Here equals there. When we have arrived there we have not left here. Supreme salvation is to be found here, or nowhere at any time. It is, and is beyond the reach and range of time or place.

Some of those present will know the Heart Sutra, recited in Japanese in temples every day, since it was first written down, we know not when, some thousand years ago. It is the quintessence of the famous *Prajnaparamita* literature, 'the Wisdom that has gone Beyond'. In those comparatively few words, all but meaningless without some commentary, is to be found all that may be said of the Void, which is void of *all things*, even of emptiness, that is both Nirvana and Samsara, an awareness already immanent or we could not achieve it. But it is also transcendent or it could not be immanent. That is why immanence and transcendence are two ways of looking at the same thing.

In Tibetan Buddhism the whole purpose of much elaborate and secret ritual is to enable the pupil to become aware of this fact, that there is nothing that his *guru* can give him. He has it. He *is* it.

In the same way, in the violent awareness of Zen, the Zen Master, in dealing with his pupil, is only concerned as quickly as possible to make the pupil understand that there is nothing that he need or can achieve and nothing that he will gain from his Master. The Master may shout at him, abuse him, laugh at him or sneer at him until the pupil with sufficient emotional and spiritual drive, intellectual ferment, intensity of will, collects the whole of his faculties and breaks out of his egg of self-induced illusion—and wonders what all the fuss was about. There is in fact nothing that we can learn, nothing that we have to achieve, save that we do not need to learn anything, and *that* takes a lot of learning!

What is the metaphysical background to that position? It is necessary to go back to basic Hinduism, to the coming forth into manifestation of that which is nameless, to *Para-Brahman*, 'beyond Brahman'. It is utterly Beyond, beyond God, or any concept of God out of which 'God' came. And in that great unrolling of the Universe, and the rolling back of that Universe, in the 'Day and Night of Brahma', there are periods of time which to us are almost inconceivable, but yet in India are calculated to the last day. Three hundred and eleven, nought forty and nine noughts (which I cannot put into words), is the calculated period of a Day and a Night of Brahma. The unrolling of the Universe onto the plain of manifestation and the rolling of it back, in that process the 'Unborn, Unoriginated, Unformed', as the Buddha called the Absolute, comes forth into the world of the born, the originated and formed. And as the great cycle begins again, we have what the Buddhists call 'the Wheel of Re-birth'. Upon this wheel each unit of life, moving down into grosser and grosser form, gathering about it sheath after sheath of matter of ever grosser type, finds itself bound by its own necessity, going round, life after life, driven by its own folly, its own blindness and its own desires, until it wakes up sufficiently, by lives and lives of suffering, to strive to break that wheel, to be freed from it, and so move off it on the path to Enlightenment.

Meanwhile, in every ultimate atom of that matter of which the Universe is made, is the One, the One Itself, emanating from THAT the Ultimate. In every minutest particle of form is life, and that life is the manifestation of the unnameable Ultimate or *Para-Brahman*. There is no death. There is only the dissolution of the form in which some aspect or ray of the one Life had until that moment manifested. Life outlives the form and breaks it by its very power. You must realize that we die, not from want of life but from too much of it, because the form can no longer contain the one, unbreakable, eternal, timeless Life. Life breaks that form and moves on. It can no longer use that form. That form is abandoned but Life goes on, and that Life or Spirit is the manifestation of the force which the Indians call just THAT or *Para-Brahman*, which the Buddhist calls the Unborn, Unoriginated, Unformed; all names are useless. But in every single 'thing' there is something of this Life, or that thing would not be there. When Life passes on to its own high purposes, to create and use and finally wear out still other forms, that form can be put into the dustbin or the incinerator or the crematorium. It is finished and has had its day. But Life goes on.

Now we will go a little higher still, to the Kegon school of Japanese Buddhism. Here we find what seems to me the supreme observation of the human mind, Jijimuge, 'the unimpeded inter-diffusion of all things or particulars'. We can understand a principle which has ten thousand manifestations. We can understand that each manifestation is, so to speak, one with its principle. But we cannot conceive how each single thing can be identical with, utterly identical with and in no sense separate from, *each other* particular. Which means that every door knob in the world is every other door knob and is every bus, and is every banana, and, because thoughts are things, is every concept. Every conceivable thing, visible and invisible, is every other conceivable thing. *All* distinctions are falsely imagined. The human mind cannot take that in as a thought, and yet one has to know it to be true.

It has been said that the Middle Way of Buddhism is a middle way which has no middle. I thought that a grand idea when it recently came to me; then I found that a Zen Master said it in 1423. But that did not trouble me because I believe that each human being, before he is perfect, will re-find for himself every single truth ever found by any other human being. Otherwise he does not *know* it. Only a few weeks ago I found that I had written in my text book *Buddhism,* in 1951, that very sentence as a profound observation of truth!

We shall all do this and we shall go on doing it, and it is pertinent to what I am saying. Here is Truth Immanent, sparkling, flashing, telling you something that you did not *know* before. In that moment you were God Immanent to say 'I *know*', but what you know has come from the Transcendent.

So much, then, for some principles and truths which pertain to transcendence. How do we *know* that Transcendence? Only because it is immanent. Hence the profound saying, 'We learn nothing. We only become aware of what we know.' No man can give another anything. Not the greatest teacher can give you anything you have not already got. We could not know one word of truth unless that truth was already immanent in the mind. In the same way the immanent as such is always transcendent. Why? Because it is only what it is because it is beyond the limitations of 'me'. 'I' at my highest, in moments of pure intuition, may be immanent enough to know the transcendent, but I am blocked in the measure of my understanding by this cursed little thing called 'me'. It is the limitations of the personality, the ego, which keeps away the light, which prevents us knowing what we are; from being what we are; which clouds our immanence. And therefore I say we can only know the transcendent by virtue of our immanence, but our immanence is always transcendent to the extent that we know it. That

which we know by the intuition we know by having struggled
out of the limitations of 'I', and in that moment our transcendence is our immanence and vice versa.

We have, therefore, to get beyond 'me'. What is this 'beyond'?
It is the only thing that matters. It is the whole purpose of the
spiritual life. The Indians, thousands of years ago, discovered
'Tat twam asi': 'Thou art THAT'. H. B. Blavatsky, trying to use
the English language to express the inexpressible, in *The Secret
Doctrine* called it 'Be-ness', as distinct from Being. There is THAT
which is in Being, has come into Being, and is now manifest.
Behind Being is Be-ness. For Christian terminology we have to
go to the supreme mind of the Christian West, Eckhart, who
alone, so far as I know, made clear that beyond 'Gott' is 'Gott-
heit'. Beyond God is Godhead, just as beyond Brahman is *Para-
Brahman*. If only we understand this fully and clearly enough,
the whole of our problems over the word 'God' or 'Not-God', go.
'God' *is*, but God is not Ultimate. Behind and beyond our concept of God, however great, is THAT from which that concept
came.

Zen Buddhists are the only people who have gone beyond the
facile remark of so many religions: 'The many will sooner or
later return to the One.' 'Maybe,' says the Zen Master, 'but
when all things are reduced to the One, to what is the One
reduced?' Because if it is not reduced, it is merely a case of the
Many/One, and there is once more a pair of opposites. Until you
can get *behind* the One *and* the Many, as Dr Suzuki is fond of
saying, 'to that point before there was a forking and a division
into two', you are still in the field of duality, and it does not
matter whether you talk of the Many or the One. They are only
a pair of opposites.

Well, what now? We are up at the level of THAT, of Be-ness,
of Godhead, *Para-Brahman*. Are we going to ask ourselves the
question: 'Why did God create the Universe?' Strangely enough
it is not such a difficult question to answer. Work it out for
yourself. The answer is: 'In order that He might know himself
to be God.' Here lies the teaching of the Supreme Sacrifice.
Absolute Perfection must become imperfect if it is to know itself.
Where there is nothing else but a total All-Consciousness, which
is All-Unconscious, where there is no differentiation or difference

whatsoever, that Thing, Person, Being—call it what you like—that Absolute knows nothing. In order to know, in order that there may be *self*-knowledge, *self*-consciousness, consciousness of itself, there must be something which is *not* that Supreme Consciousness. In other words, the Absolute must manifest and create a shadow of itself in order that it may know itself to be what it is, the Absolute. That is the Ultimate Mystery, the ultimate, intensely exciting spiritual Awareness. That God Himself must sacrifice Himself in order to be God. How much more must we, who are rays, flames of the light of God, sacrifice ourselves if we would know ourselves to be God and say, 'I am'.

What can we do to see this Immanence, to know what we are? Buddhists would say: 'Let die out for want of fuelling the Three Fires which at present burn unceasingly in every human heart; hatred, lust and illusion.' Hatred as a sense of difference, a sense of attraction to things we like, of repulsion for what we do not like, a sense of distinction between the various forms of life. Desire, in every conceivable form, for self. For a greater 'self', for the family. For a larger unit still, the company, the job, the club, the society, the nation. It is still desire. Desire for some part against the will and purpose of the Ultimate Whole. So long as that desire exists and is manifest there must be war. There must be mutual killing, destruction and death. There can be no spiritual awareness. Only when that fire is allowed to die for want of fuelling do we begin to see what we are. And as for illusion, the basic illusion I have described, the belief that there is any distinction or difference, remember that '*all* distinctions are falsely imagined'.

Let us see where this is taking us. It means that this Path which we so glibly talk about, whether we call it the 'Noble Eight-fold Path' or the 'Sermon on the Mount', is the road to self-suicide, for we shall not reach the end of that path until we, as self, have learnt to die. To die to all at present we hold most dear. To die in the death of the very thing for which at present we fight and strive so strenuously day by day. The 'I' that wants this, will not have that, will not be pushed about and is quite determined to become the boss of the business. The 'I' that wants a larger car, and everything else in sight, and will not have its own desires frustrated or thwarted by anything alive. Until *that* dies, there will be no progress, for the end of the journey is the death of 'I'. It is worth considering therefore, what is this 'I' that treads this path, because if it is only 'me', you will not get far. Why not? Because 'me' is going to do everything that it can to stop 'I' from getting to the end of that path, because it knows that progress is a process of self-suicide.

Meanwhile, we *are* Enlightened. We have this truth immanent. We have it, so what are we going to do? Let us try for a moment to behave *as if* it were true. If it *is* true, and we make the effort to live accordingly, much will happen. First, and all I am going to mention here, there will come the awakening of compassion. I use the word compassion, which is so much greater than 'love', for love today is such an abused term. Compassion has nothing to do with the desires of the self *for* the self; it is as great as Wisdom and is so regarded in Buddhism. Prajna, supreme Wisdom, Karuna, Supreme Compassion, are described as one, two aspects of the same Reality. There can be no Wisdom until Compassion for all living things is commensurate. There can be no true Compassion which is not given the eyes of wisdom, so that it may work usefully and not against the common will. Therefore compassion must be awakened before the eyes of wisdom can see. We shall not *see* Immanence until we have dedicated our lives for the greater part to the pursuit and happiness of our fellow men. Only as we cease to work for self, and work for the 'Greater Self', will there be room for awareness within of the mighty purpose of the universe. Only then do we gain some glimpse of the next impersonal job to be done. There is no need to trouble why, or when, or how. That knowledge will come. An impersonal job to be done each moment of the day is surely a finer way of life than that of most of us, which is to gain for ourselves or to retain for ourselves as much as we can in the face of the needs of others.

In the Buddhist East there is the complementary ideal of the Bodhisattva and the Arhat, the Arhat predominantly working for his own perfection on the ground that he is the one person whose mind he can perfect, the Bodhisattva working for all mankind, because he cannot be bothered about himself. Of course they are complementary. Only the man who is working for others will achieve results for himself. On the other hand, you cannot achieve results for others if you are not working to improve and in the end perfect yourself.

We must learn to *feel* the Beyond within ourselves. We can, if we like, use ritual, or prayer or devotion or meditation. Or we can, surprisingly enough, do without the lot because we are just too busy, because there are too many things to be done at the moment for the helping of other people. We can say, in Christian terminology, 'Not my will but Thine be done'. Why? Because in immanence 'I' and 'My Father' are One. And when 'I' am working wholeheartedly, impersonally, for some other person or thing, I *am* my Father. My immanence *is* my transcendence. There is no separate self, as the Buddha pointed out a thousand times over. Analyze the thing called self. Is there anything permanent, and different from any other body, in any part of it? In my physical body, in my emotions, in my mental reactions? In my ideals and convictions and hopes and fears and principles? Or even in *my* consciousness? No. There is even no such thing as *my* consciousness. There is consciousness, aware at the moment of the illusion of 'I'. There is nothing that is mine that is not yours. There is nothing permanently 'me'. That which in me is common to the whole world is not mine. All that is mine alone is not the Divine Immanence. To the extent that I am in a state of consciousness of my own immanence, I have transcended myself and am no longer concerned with 'me'. Surely it is obvious, when you come to think of it, there can be no separate, immortal soul. The very concept is nonsense, demonstrably untrue. And yet on that rock Christianity has, I believe, largely foundered. It is a trgically wrong description of what was never taught by Christ, even as the *anatta* doctrine taught today in some of the schools of Theravada Buddhism has no basis in the Buddhist Scriptures. The Buddha never said 'there is no self' and Christ never said 'each man has *an* immortal soul which distinguishes him for ever from any other immortal soul'. Spirit *is*. A billion souls *are*, and each has a body. There is your Pauline Trinity, and I accept it. Spirit is one. Souls—for want of a better term—are many, and they have bodies and personalities which perish. But the Spirit is One, and the Spirit in any two men is the same Spirit.

All the great religions of the world speak of a path, a path of ethics and much beside. Some tread that path as mystics, some as occultists, the man of spiritual vision or the spiritual scientist. The mystic gains a glimpse with his intuition of the light at the top of Everest, and moves as best he can, through the darkness between, towards that light. The occultist, the spiritual scientist, says, 'I notice that the ground is rising. I see in front of me a step. I will take that step, examine it, test it, look to its under-pinning, make sure that it is sound. I will then take another step and consolidate that.' He and the mystic may reach the top at the same time, but their temperaments are different. The intro-vert and the extrovert, again, take complementary paths. In Zen Buddhism there are the rival schools of the 'gradual' and the 'sudden' methods of achieving Enlightenment. Zen, as a school, is unique. It is historically an attempt to get back to that which made 'Buddhism', which was the Buddha's Enlightenment. But the Buddha had no scriptures, no apparatus and he needed no ritual of any kind. He trod a path. He found the goal of it. He taught all men the path to that goal, and he said to each of his disciples, 'Tread it'. Zen Buddhism was founded as a revulsion from the metaphysical subtleties of Indian thought by a man of mighty but uncommon sense who said, 'Put the lot in the dust-bin. Stop all this ritual and the like. You *are* Buddha, Enlighten-ment (or whatever word you like). Get up and behave accord-ingly.' And the 'sudden' method of Zen is the sudden burst through to that awareness. But whatever the technique, what-ever the nation, whatever the age, whatever the name of the so-called religion, always one comes back to this, and it is my last word as a Buddhist. There is no distinction between trans-cendence and immanence; any imagined distinction is false and is itself a way of preventing each human being becoming aware of the Transcendent Immanence in his own mind.

Beyond

Beyond the compass of the day, beyond
The unfettered flight of rising thought, which sings
And soars, wide-throated in delight, with bliss
Of bright awareness; utterly beyond
The wildest reach of far imagining,
Is what? The mind expands, intolerant
Of all unknowing, builds and nobly dreams
Of ultimates of bold infinity;
In vain. The stallions of enquiry storm
The blue-lit fields of high philosophy
In vain. Thought falters, founders in despair,
With empty hands admitting impotence.

Science; the word is stuffed with arrogance.
The power of mind; here's thought gone mad with self.
The heart; here's better bludgeon for the door
That bars Reality. Frail water slow
Dissolves the living and tremendous rock
Into oblivion. Shall the heart with soft
Relentless will consume the rampart walls
Of self, the folly self? Here's hope in vain;
For thought and feeling, twins of reasoning
Spring from the loins of dull duality.
Not this, not with a weapon in the hand
That thrusts at something other, not with two
In bitter contest is this battle won,
But sudden, when the friend is foe and each
Dissolved in each, ceases to be.
                                    What then?
What notches cut to climb, what rising path
To fresh awareness? How to *know* beyond
All acquisition, loss or difference?
The printed word is but a burden now,
Speech but a sound unmeaning on the air.
Not here, not there, but somewhere, casket-hidden,
Truth, ere man arose to seek, ere time
Had semblance, *is*, unmoving, unconfined . . .

It is within. Here's heart of all enquiry.
Here, not at the goal of far adventure,
Now, not in the long convenience of time;
And doing this, though this be pale of worth
And fruitless to mankind. It flames, it shines,
A light-house light that in the hands of will
Burns with awareness . . .

                  Such is fancy still;
Projected image on projected screen;
Here's nought to see of true experience.
Still the machine of thought is sounding. Still,
Recording nothing worth, the folded sheets
Of knowledge clatter through. What function, then,
What process of im-mediate consciousness
Shall tear the mask from seeming, break each mould
And thus let life, all body shed, be free?

It is the voice of Truth invisible,
A lamp in every human mind, the light
That glows upon the darkling road to heaven.
It knows the substance of beyond, and shines
In darkness, downward, to illume the sad
Arena of our proud self-consciousness;
And up, a searchlight in the sun, with rays
Of pure experience. By this alone
We know direct, as one who sudden looks
Into the face of God and, letting fall
The burden, loses self-awareness. Reason
Then, refused the final view may yet
Create a desperate ladder to the height,
And, even as the feet that climb let fall
The steps of their arrival, so shall thought
Be servant to a nobler faculty
In forfeit of attainment. Let us climb.

Life is of THAT—we know It not, nor shall—
The Namelessness, the Void, God's Father. Men
Have mouthed a thousand names for It, nor stained
It with the sound. We see the robes that clothe
Its first becoming, attributes of power
And such dimension as the strutting mind

Can fold about Infinity. We cry,
With folded hands of pitiful demand
And desperate invocation. Yet we know—
And here's an infant candle in the night
Of ignorance—that all that breathes is part
And child of this magnificence. If, then,
(The voice of thought breaks in with argument)
The Absolute is knowable as One
And in the One the ceaseless manifold,
Shall not the littlest part of Wholeness see,
Attain, become the like Divinity?

Alas that thought has no such knowing. Thought,
Which measures, tears each petal from the rose
Whose loveliness, intangible as dawn
Laughs at the scalpel of enquiry. Thought
Proclaims, and splendidly, that 'Thou art THAT'
Yet utter fails to see the Darkness-Light
Made visible. Be humble now; the eye
Intuitive has no dimensions, knows
And absolutely, sees with instant power
Of eyeless vision—suddenly to see,
Direct, none seeing, utterly aware.

Beyond—the word is failing. Now the Truth
Exultant as a rocket, shatters the gates
Of wonder. There's no heaven yonder save
The heaven here, no hell but evil wrought
Of man's devising. There is nought beyond!

Thus Wisdom throned in self-identity,
In non-duality of earth and heaven,
Burns and blends and fuses all that's two
And in their suchness sees them utterly
At once divided-indivisible.
Wisdom expands; Compassion, as a flower
That, delicately waking, swells from bud
To blossom in the warm and love-lit air,
With swift, consummate skill-in-means commands
A thousand forms of helpfulness. Wisdom-
Compassion, each the majesty of each,
Twin pulses of the heart of being, grow
In fusion of dissolved communion.

Where reason falters, discord in a surge
Of meaning shatters the pregnant stillness
Into sudden joy. So Truth, with noise
Of merriment explodes the One, scatters
A thousand petals on the laughing air
And thunders in the streets of our illusion.
The tempest shrivels. There is utter light
In silence visible. A vast content
Made luminous consumes awareness. Thought,
Bereft of purpose, lightless, impotent
Abandons effort in a wild despair.
The search is ended; there is no beyond,
Save in the vast immeasurable bliss,
Beyond beyond, of here and now and this.

Zen Buddhism

22

The Approach to Zen

The school of Zen may be viewed as part of the Mahayana School or entirely on its own. It uses all scriptures and is bound by none, and likewise uses any technique or means (*upaya*) which serves its end, which is to awaken the pupil's mind to its own Enlightenment. But whatever its genesis or place in the Buddhist field it is unique in the long record of religious history. As a force it was responsible for the greatest art of China, and much of the finest culture of China and Japan. It has produced in those countries some of their greatest minds. Yet when describing Zen, and the history and technique of the school of Zen, it is easy to give a totally wrong impression, both of Zen and the school which seeks it. To regard it as so much 'fun and games', as witty nonsense or paradox gone mad, is to confuse the finger which points at the moon with the moon at which it points. These strange, provocative methods of speech and behaviour occur, it is true, in the course of transmission of Zen; they are not of its substance.

Yet the history of Zen may help to convey its nature and place in the Buddhist field. In India, where Buddhism was born, we find as already explained that not long after the Buddha's passing the exuberant Indian mind developed, from the original teaching, a magnificent range of brilliant and profound thought, and with it some of the world's greatest philosophers. This new philosophy went further East, and finally reached China. But the Chinese were not impressed with this wordy statement of Reality, and even more disliked the Sangha, because its members

begged for food and did no work for their living. The Chinese
are a practical, earth-minded race, and believe that every man
should work out his own salvation with diligence—in the fields.

This resistance was broken down in the sixth century A.D. by
Bodhidharma, who was born of noble family in South India. He
became one of the most advanced thinkers of his day, and in due
course travelled to China. When he arrived, his reputation had
preceded him, and he was invited to visit the Emperor of that
day. The interview was most unusual. After the usual ceremony
of the ancient Chinese Court, the Emperor began to boast of his
many achievements for his people. He said:

'I have built many temples and monasteries, I have copied the
sacred books. Now what is my merit?'
Bodhidharma replied: 'None whatever, Sire.'
The Emperor, taken aback, enquired: 'What is to be con-
sidered the first principle of the Dharma?'
Bodhidharma replied: 'Vast Emptiness and nothing holy
therein.'
Asked the Emperor, not unreasonably: 'Who, then, is it who
stands before me?'
'I have no idea,' said Bodhidharma.

That, whether true or not, is an epigrammatic way of describing China's reaction to the verbiage of Indian Buddhism, and
Zen, or Ch'an to use the original name, has been rightly
described as China's reaction to the Buddhism which came from
India. What by the Indian mind was expressed in numerous
volumes was, in China, compressed into a single sentence. Indian
philosophy spoke at length of the Absolute. In China it was
expressed thus: 'What,' asked a pupil, 'is the One word of
Reality?' Answer: 'You make it two.' The mode of expression,
and hence of the transmission of experience, was in this way
lifted from the plane of the intellect to the realm of super-
consciousness which lies beyond concepts of any kind.

The ebullience of Indian thought was thus, from the Zen point
of view, a decline from the spiritual heights at which the Buddha
taught, and Chinese influence served to produce a reversion to
its original, direct simplicity. After all, Buddhism is *Buddh*-ism,

the 'ism' or school of *buddh*, the Buddha's Awakening. All else now known as Buddhism has developed, with more or less excuse, from the one supreme experience which raised a man to Buddhahood. It follows that to drag from their grandiloquent heights the speculations of Indian philosophy was a move in the right direction. If so, the school of Zen is nearer than any other to the Light, and has the most right to be called the school of Buddha's Enlightenment.

What, then, is Zen? The answer is simple. It is the Buddha's Enlightenment, the Buddha's spiritual achievement attained as the guerdon of a thousand lives completely dedicated to that end. It follows that to know what is Buddhism, and therefore Zen, one must achieve the Buddha's experience. Anything less is less than Zen. The process of Enlightenment begins here and now, with this, whatever is now in hand. The rest is a process of the mind's expansion until consciousness becomes commensurate at will with that which lies beyond imagining.

The Buddha was a man, not God, and his teaching was plain. 'This have I found—Suffering and the Way to the end of suffering. Where I have trodden all may tread. Work out your own salvation, with diligence.' That is reasonable. It is equally reasonable to speak of steps on the long path up the mountain to self-enlightenment. We are now on the valley floor. Perhaps we think that, having news of the summit, we are on the way. But are we? Are we even in training for the climb? If we go into training, learn the technique of climbing, study the way on maps (prepared by previous climbers), and develop the will to achieve success we shall at least be ready to climb. We know, for the Buddha has told us, what we shall find upon the way, but we shall not know the nature of the summit until we get there. But if we begin to climb, at least into the foothills, our vision will expand; we shall see more of the sunlight and more of the way. If we climb a little higher we shall see still more, but if we stay in our chairs and discuss the thoughts of others *about* the way, we shall stay, as most of us do stay, in our chairs. There is no lift up this mountain. Let us begin, then, to climb.

There are two ways of climbing; in a spiral, gently, by degrees; or fiercely, directly, straight. The first is the usual Buddhist way; the second, the 'sudden' way, is Zen. Bodhidharma is said to have laid down four propositions of Zen. 'A special transmission outside the Scriptures; no dependence upon words; direct pointing to the Mind of man; seeing into one's own nature and the attainment of Buddhahood.' That is clear enough, and is made the simpler by the maddening logic of Zen. If you want to climb a mountain, begin at the top. But is this advice so strange to Western ears? Did not Jesus say, 'Seek ye first the Kingdom of God, and all things shall be added unto you'? The journey, the change from this to that, is illusion. Only the Here is real and the Here is Now and This. The process lies in the mind, and the whole of circumstance is the field wherein to become aware of our own inherent bliss.

The approach to Zen is total, using the whole man. In the West we abide by logic, the instrument of the thinking mind. 'This being so, that is so; that being so, this follows.' In the East the approach is not in a straight line of argument, but from every point of view at once, and each of them direct. Truth, to be utterly absorbed and known, must be grasped by the whole man, using his instruments of sense, emotion, thought and intuition, and all other means which enable a man to grasp the Absolute. For Zen, like mysticism and pure philosophy, seeks the One, but seeks it differently. 'The Many returns to the One. So be it, but to what does the One return?' What would the mystics say to that? Zen goes into the One and out of it, for Zen is the Many and the One, the living experience which transcends the distinctions of the mind. In terms of psychology, the Self which *knows* is born on the margin of the conscious and unconscious, and thereafter as it grows absorbs both equally. In terms of philosophy, the pilgrim treads a Middle Way between all extremes, but in Zen the straight and narrow way folds up to a point and the point is nowhere to be found. It is the centre of a circle whose circumference is everywhere, a circle whose centre is nowhere: it lives in the 'one thought-moment' beyond space and time. Always in life the moments that matter are where thought ends; they appear in nonsense, as lightning in sunlight, as a burst of laughter over a cup of tea. 'Usual life is very Tao,' said a Master of Zen. But the usual life in which Zen shines is most unusual. It must be found if at all in daily life, or 'daily life' is out of the field of Zen, and Zen would not be Zen.

For Zen is that which, in modern parlance, makes life tick, and will therefore appear in our daily 'chores' as frequently and brightly as in meditation under a tree. It will not be found only in peculiar robes or peculiar positions. And why? Because *satori*, the flash of enlightening, happens in the mind, and the mind is equally with us in the temple, the office and the lavatory. Only in our self-wrought circumstance will Zen appear, and even then when all distinction of holy and unholy Zen and not-Zen is destroyed.

The process of finding it involves what Jung calls the withdrawal of projections. There must be no running away from life, still less from Zen. Yet men attempt to escape in many ways. They escape into pleasure, phantasy, superstition; into slothful inactivity, detective stories, hobbies, dreams; into concepts that are a substitute for reality. They run away into illness, moodiness, insanity and death. Why? Because they fear the Reality they loudly claim to seek. Psychologists say that many of their patients' troubles arise from 'refused fear'. They know that they are afraid but fear to face the cause of it, the thing they fear. So they run from life while Zen delights in it, all parts of it, and laughs, not at it, for that implies duality, but with it as it sings and ripples and flows. It follows that in Zen it does not matter who or what we are; still less does it matter what we do, so long as we learn from the effects of what we do, which is in turn the consequence of what we are. How do we react to circumstance? With fear, or Zen?

The ways of approach to Zen are infinite; they are not confined to Japan, and there may be in time a Western school of Zen. The Japanese Rinzai School makes much use of the *koan*, a word or phrase which has no sense, no meaning. The most famous of all is 'mu', an absolute 'no' or 'not'. At this moment in Japan there are probably five thousand monks in fierce, unremitting concentration on some such *koan* as 'Two hands make a sound of clapping. What is the sound of one?' The *mondo* is nearly as meaningless to our concept-ridden minds. It is a rapid question-answer, a kind of shorthand conversation between the pupil and the Master's highly trained and illumined mind, by which the pupil is helped to smash the limitations of thought, and to break through to the absolute point of view. The question may sound foolish, yet it is put in deadly earnest; the answer is always nonsense to the intellect. It may be a smile, a gesture, silence or a blow. If the pupil misses the point the Master tries again, and probably more violently. Anything, just anything is used and justified which raises the pupil's mind above duality, to the absolute awareness which transcends it. The limitation of all concept, which of its nature works by comparison, must be utterly broken before the pupil can genuinely say 'I know'.

What, then, is Zen? Your answer is as good as mine, for there is none. The word is the Japanese corruption, via the Chinese Ch'an, of the Sanskrit term Dhyana, vaguely translated as meditation. Its meaning is the meaning of all life, for it is that which lies behind manifestation, and is therefore to us the Absolute. To know it while on earth is the supreme paradox and the supreme act of truth. None can reveal it, none conceal it. Asked by a pupil to reveal the essence of Buddhism, the Master replied by taking the pupil for a walk in the woods. They came to a bush of wild laurel in bloom. 'There,' said the Master, 'you think I am concealing something from you. There is the essence of Buddhism.' Nor can a man see Zen or handle it. 'How when a man brings nothing with him?' asked a pupil. 'Throw it away,' said the Master. 'What shall I throw when I am not burdened at all?' 'If so, bring it along.'

Zen lives in facts and hates abstractions. It therefore hates all concepts, as so many cages in which the flow of life is foolishly confined. Asked what is Buddhism, a Master replied, 'I do not understand Buddhism'. Why should he? Is not the dawn and the singing of a bird, and the taste of tea and the touch of jade the direct experience of Reality? If not, what is? Zen is the flow of the river, and we on either bank shout loudly that the other is wrong. We cling to the banks who fear the flowing; we fear to live who fear to flow. Zen is in laughter and song and immediate acceptance. It refuses nothing, being all. It knows no good or evil for all is Good; nor ugliness where all is Beautiful. Above the dualities invented by men's minds is the absolute 'right' which in our hearts we know and in our brains is clouded with opinion. He who accepts the moment finds the eternal moment, and in that Now all is and all is right. In the world of illusion we live by the laws and the moral codes of men; the mind of the Zen-illumined is free, not only of the bonds of love and hate and thinking but even of the notion that the mind is free. Such men have vision in their eyes, compassion in their every act. They know, and in their certainty show forth the heart's serenity. Not pausing to argue or define they just walk on unceasingly into error and out of it, uphill or down, and over a precipice if that is the forward way. When self is not, who suffers hurt from things? When hate and lust and illusion die in the mind from want of fuelling, what is there left but laughter and understanding, and a gentle walking on? Whither do they walk? To no-where for there is only Here. No matter, for in the Zen-filled mind there is neither this nor that nor the folly of now and then. Away, then, with solemnity and the desperate wrestling of the concept-laden mind. Let go, of everything (although, as I have said elsewhere, it needs great courage to let go). Then what happens? 'The Light is within thee,' said the Egyptian Hierophants. 'Let the Light shine.' 'There is no difference between an enlightened and an unenlightened man,' said the Patriarch Hui-neng, 'save that the one knows that he is enlightened, and the other does not.'

Zen, then, is in the here and now, and the right doing of this. It is to be found in the right posting of a letter or washing up. If not, it will not be found. Zen is the act of walking on, but there is no path, no walker and no goal. You say that this is nonsense. So it is, but it is super-sense, an awareness shared by the poet, the lover and the child. And also by the self-enlightened man. The intellect is a brilliant tool, but when the river is crossed the raft is left behind. Thoughts should be servants. In the West they become our masters, and bind us on our sojourning. Asked by a pupil to set him free, the Master replied, 'Who puts you under restraint?' Was the Buddha's Enlightenment merely splendid thinking, or the act of reunion of the part with the Whole, the conscious with the unconscious mind, that freedom when the self, in dying, learns that it is free? Asked 'What is Zen?' the Master replied, 'Walk on'.

23

On Breaking Through

When an Indian prince, seated in rags under the Bo Tree, shattered 'the ridge-pole of the house of self', and his consciousness expanded to the confines of the universe, he proclaimed himself and was accepted as *Buddha*, the Enlightened One. What he taught, for the benefit of those 'whose eyes were scarcely covered with any dust', was a Way, 'from desire to peace' as the Lama said in Kipling's *Kim*, from the darkness of our present mind to the full light of Enlightenment.

It surely follows that nothing in the field of Buddhist literature or training is of the least worth unless it points to, and helps the Buddhist nearer to, the same Enlightenment.

But a Path implies progress along it, and expansion of the mind which treads this inner Way. Such progress is 'gradual', meaning step by step. Is this Way but a journey at some stage on which will come a 'sudden' flash of Enlightenment, or is it a planned, deliberate process of increasing expansion of consciousness which will in time achieve, *or bring the mind to a point when it is ripe for achieving*, the first flash of the Light on its own plane, that of the Absolute?

Japanese Buddhists call this Kensho, a 'first showing', and maintain, I understand, that it need have no relation to the student's moral development or learning, need not produce any visible change in character or conduct, and is in fact no more than evidence that his efforts are focused in the right direction. These flashes increase in frequency, quality and magnitude (if such terms have any meaning in this context) until the first

Satori, or major 'break-through' rewards the questing mind.

The simile of a 'break-through' implies a mind self-fettered with its own past thought and feeling, which beats upon a wall created by such thinking, and strives to break through the wall to the realm of Non-duality. In the West, the strongest of these fetters, the most unyielding concept, is the illusion that thought, however strong or clear, can of itself directly *know* the Truth, as distinct from learning more and more about it. It cannot. *The Voice of the Silence* says, 'the Mind is the great Slayer of the Real. Let the Disciple slay the Slayer.' Only Buddhi, in the West called intuition, the built-in faculty which, as the reflection of 'the Unborn, Unoriginated, Unformed' is the Light of the Unborn shining within, can penetrate this well-cemented wall of false belief and *know,* directly, face to face, Reality.

What effort, training or achieved condition of mind, if any, will produce this first awareness of No-thought, of Non-duality? I do not know. We read in the Zen Scriptures of the 'moment' of enlightenment of men who later became masters, and in the West we are accumulating information of what seem to be genuine experiences, great or small, occurring year by year in Western minds. What have the latter in common? It is too early to say, but most of the persons concerned had never heard of Zen. Nearly all had newly passed through a period of inward strain which 'broke' in Kensho, but what did these people 'do' which, if anything, was the 'cause' of a 'break-through'? Nothing, it seems, deliberately, though most had developed 'a strong spirit of enquiry', as the Zen masters call it, and strenuously sought the Beyond of thought and feeling.

Then what can we do, here and now, in the West, if anything, to achieve, or induce, a Zen experience? I repeat that I do not know, but I firmly believe that we can do much to prepare the mind for such experience, and to bring nearer the 'moment' when it will 'suddenly' occur. I appreciate the remark of one of my own Class; 'we are not here to improve the ego but to kill it,' but the deliberate self-training which I advocate and try to practise is itself a means of 'killing' or 'letting go' the ego. Let me elaborate what I have in mind, and have taught the Zen Class of the Society for thirtyfive years. If I am wrong I hope to be told so, from Europe or Japan.

I accept that there is no conceivable relation between the relative and the Absolute, between duality and Non-duality. It follows that the least 'break-through' is an event beyond time and space as we conceive them, beyond description and therefore beyond the reach of 'proof', and incommunicable save to a mind which has itself already broken through.

But I believe, from my own experience, that, independent of any occasional peeps of Non-Duality, there can be and should be a planned and steady development of 'character' in the three departments of the Eightfold Path, doctrinal study ('views'), morality (*sila*) and mind-expansion, preferably in that order, towards a clearly perceived and purposed end. I accept again that the Buddhist is not concerned with improving the self but with dropping it, but the truth of this depends on the spelling of self. Of the illusion-born and separative self or 'ego' this is true. Of the SELF, the 'Unborn, Unoriginated, Unformed', which manifests in Life in all its forms and dwells in all of us, it cannot be true, else what achieves a break-through to an already possessed Enlightenment? But what of the Self, 'above' the self but 'below' the SELF, 'that which is reborn from life to life' by the force of karma, which is itself perishable but, during the treading of the Way, to be clearly distinguished from the self or ego? Can this not be purified, developed, ennobled, and so raised towards its innate Buddhic consciousness, and is this not the very purpose of the Path, however named? If I am right, this is something that all of us may do in daily life in preparation for Zen experience. As the mind is progressively controlled, the heart expanded with compassion, the clamour of self diminished, and habitual thought uplifted (yes, an excellent term) to 'higher', more spiritual states of awareness, the whole field of the mind, of thought and feeling, aspiration and habitual consciousness, is increasingly illumined by Enlightenment, even as the sun progressively breaks through the morning mist and dissolves the night into the cloudless light of day.

Such is a fair description of noble minds that I have met, men who had never heard of Zen nor, so far as I learnt, ever known a Zen 'experience'. Here, I believe, on the highest levels of the thinking mind, great writers, thinkers, poets, musicians; great scientists and statesmen and religious teachers, the truly 'great' minds of any race or clime are illumined by the same light, the indivisible, omnipresent light of Enlightenment.

Are these no nearer Kensho than you or I? I believe they are. Zen philosophy is based on the doctrine of the Void and the mystical awareness of the 'Buddha within', and it is self alone, and the 'three fires' of hatred, lust and illusion that burn within it, that prevent us seeing and becoming this Buddhic principle within the Plenum-Void. It surely follows that as the thinking mind is more and more illumined, the faculty of Buddhi, intuition, is the more developed and aroused to 'see', and when the last screen falls the 'gradual' process of the mind's enlightenment is crowned with 'sudden' experience.

In Japan, I understand, there is no such preparation in this form. The student in search of enlightenment is immediately taught to 'sit', first physically, then with concentration on the breathing, and then with a koan to occupy his entire attention until 'solved' in the field of Non-Duality. In the West we do not use the koan, and it would be foolish to do so in the absence of a Roshi able to control its use. What then should we do? I submit as above, that we should so lift the habitual level of mind that it is more and more illumined in its field of thought until the intuition, waiting for the 'moment' when thought as such can go no further, suddenly breaks through.

True, this process omits the unconscious mind in its psychological sense, and the purpose of the koan technique, I understand, is so to still the thinking mind that the contents of the unconscious may rise into consciousness, be fully faced, accepted, and then 'digested'. Is this necessary for the first Zen experience? If so, what are we to say of the cases of 'breaking through' apparently achieved, in increasing numbers, in Europe and the USA?

Let me summarize. I believe that the student of Zen in search of 'the Wisdom which lies beyond' thought, can so prepare his mind, that slowly but steadily he moves, as it were, into the field of Enlightenment. To use a final simile, above the room in which thought functions in duality is a ceiling made of that very thought. Zen training aims at breaking through this ceiling, somehow or other, and I believe that deliberate effort can little by little work on the lower surface of the ceiling until but a wafer stands between our vision and the (ever-existing) Light.

The advantage of this process must be obvious. When Kensho comes, the trained and developed mind stands steady, digests and uses the new-found Wisdom wisely, with right motive, and is ready for the next and maybe greater experience.

And then? It must never be forgotten that Kensho is the beginning of the Zen Path and not the end. For enlightenment, great or small, is to be 'used' in daily life, each hour of it, precisely in proportion as it is achieved, and the right purpose of such use is described in that handbook of the Way, *The Voice of the Silence*, 'The first step is to live to benefit mankind'.

Jijimuge

Each thing of beauty, each unlovely thing
Is other, every other, but the mind,
Thought-laden, ego-burdened and confined
With difference wrought of false imagining,
Is million-eyed to broken circumstance
And mirrors all in multiplicity.

Yet each is utter each, complicity
Of substance fusing life; no child of chance
But rightly thus, and lit with suchness, such
Beyond of difference as silence knows,
Or love, that lingers in the heart's repose
While master of the tools of sight and touch.

Each thing is void, a flung thought of illusion,
Yet dwells in unimpeded full diffusion.

24

Just So

In the Tao Tê Ching it is written, 'Those who know do not speak; those who speak do not know'. Yet many who know have spoken, and I must bear witness, though humbly, of what I know that I know, even if I do not fully understand it.

Now, Buddhism implies three propositions. First, the Buddha's Enlightenment or Awakening, by which he became the Buddha, the All-Enlightened One, the All-Compassionate One, and the Way which he taught to that Enlightenment. This is a blend of doctrine and practice. Secondly, this Middle Way is entirely subjective—it lies within. It is a method of mind-control and mind-expansion beyond the limits of our present consciousness. Thirdly, at some stage on the Path the conscious mind begins to assimilate the unconscious, whether regarded as the metaphysical 'Unborn, Unoriginated, Unformed', or the 'unconscious' of Western psychology. The relative must consume the absolute, and we must become, in Dr Suzuki's words, 'consciously unconscious'. At that stage there is no more duality, for that which creates the duality of this and that, the self, is dead.

As already said, this Light is shining now, within. As the Egyptian hierophants of old proclaimed, 'The Light is within thee; let the Light shine'. Or, in the words of The Voice of the Silence, 'Look within; thou art Buddha'.

And yet we seek it, seek it everywhere. We seek it by logic. I quote again from the Udana, for this is the basic teaching of Buddhism, as of all the world's wisdom. 'There is, O Bhikkhus, an Unborn, Unoriginated, Unformed. If there were not, there could not be an escape from the born, the originated, the formed. But because there is the Unborn . . . there is an escape from the world of the born, the originated, the formed!' This is logic, but we cannot live on logical assertions. Again, the East has sought for supernal states of mind by metaphysics. In the literature of the Prajna-paramita, 'the Wisdom that has gone beyond', we read of the ultimate and absolute Void, a voidness of all 'things' both seen and unseen, so empty that it is void of emptiness— the absolute Negative out of which the positive appearance of Samsara, the world about us, was evolved, or came. Out of THAT, as the Hindus call it, came the Oneness, which is the highest that we in duality can 'know'. Then the One divides and trembles into Two, and so is born the bi-polar field of becoming, the myriad pairs of opposites of spirit-matter, in-breathing and out-breathing, positive and negative, night and day. And out of Two comes Three for we cannot conceive Two without the relationship between them, and out of Three comes what the Chinese call 'the ten thousand things'. Now we must find our way back, to the basic Trinity, to Duality, to the One behind that and then ask ourselves, 'When all returns to the One, to what does the One return', and find the answer. Again, the mystics of all faiths have sought it, and all achieve the same experience. Intellectuals take these experiences and tabulate them, pigeon-hole them and so destroy them, but the experience on its own plane is absolute to the man who attains it: it is beyond the reach of the intellect, of any scholar's or of his own.

The West has contributed to the search. The great astronomer Jeans, in a memorable passage wrote, 'Today, there is a wide measure of agreement that the stream of knowledge is heading towards a non-mechanical reality. The universe begins to look more like a great thought than a great machine. Mind no longer appears as an accidental intruder into the realms of matter. We are beginning to suspect that we ought rather to hail it as the creator and governor of the realms of matter!' One is minded to compare this with the first verse of the Dhammapada, 'All that we are is the result of what we have thought . . . ' But in terms of the universe this 'thought' is No-thought, No-mind.

Psychology has its own contribution to the search. Carl Jung, one of the greatest of modern minds, discovered that the Self, as he called it, is born where two circles touch, that of the ego-consciousness, which one may call the Not-Self, and the Unconscious. Strangely enough, at the same time Dr Suzuki was in Japan describing the same discovery as it belongs to Buddhist philosophy. I repeat, as my third proposition of Buddhism, that consciousness must finally absorb both conscious and unconsciousness, the relative and absolute, the part and the whole.

Now all this points to a Beyond. This is the 'God-head' of Eckhart, which is behind and beyond any conception, however great, of God. It points to one Life, functioning through a million million forms; to one Law which 'moves to Good' beyond the variations of good/evil, on the relative plane; to a Whole, an unbreakable Harmony, which none can disturb or destroy with impunity, for any disharmony will recoil upon him who caused it as an adjustment, however painful, to be made. It points to the 'nothing between' of the Tao Te Ching and of mathematics, which Mrs L. C. Beckett has described in her comparison of the Lankavatara Sutra and modern astronomy.[1]

It is a Beyond, which is eternally Here and Now and This—for we only know here; it is always now and we know but this. But here and now and this, ever differing, ever the same, have this in common, that each is 'just so', in its suchness as it is and not otherwise.

But these are thoughts and we must rise beyond thoughts. All this is the springboard to experience. We must now leave doctrine behind, and the arguments and the learning of the human intellect. From now on only experience will prevail, what a man in his own mind develops, achieves, becomes. There will be flashes of Light which come unbidden, suddenly, and which will not with any effort of will be made to come again. Flashes of different value, length and breadth and shape. They begin to affect the higher mind and to irradiate its thinking. Many of us have these small experiences; only a few achieve the great breakthrough which is, however, the beginning and not the end of the final path to enlightenment.

Those who have had experience, great or small, seem to agree upon three results in the mind. First, an ever increasing serenity; then a remarkable sense of certainty, a sureness of touch in

[1] *Neti, Neti.* L. C. Beckett. Ark Press. 1955.

action, an unthought-out skill in means. As our friend Phiroz Mehta said to us once, 'Only the skilled thing is good'. Thirdly comes a sense of infinite, impersonal power to cope with what karma brings us to be done, which may be drawn upon at will so long it is unstained by self. It is, as we need it, knowledge, power, courage, patience, an ability to stand at the centre and at the same time to 'walk on' unceasingly.

Now we know something of Prajna, supreme Wisdom, but it is but the half of the whole. As Dr Suzuki has written, 'the Mahayana rests upon the twin pillars of supreme Wisdom and supreme Compassion, and the two are one'. Wisdom is imperfect until within it is born 'the great compassionate heart' which, seeing all things and beings as likewise illusionary manifestations of the same one Life, knows them to be one, without distinction, separation or difference. May I offer what I believe to be the most beautiful words ever penned in the English language? 'Let thy soul lend its ear to every cry of pain like as the lotus bares its heart to drink the morning sun. Let not the fierce sun dry one tear of pain before thyself hast wiped it from the sufferer's eye. But let each burning human tear drop on thy heart, and there remain, nor ever brush it off until the pain that caused it is removed.' [1] Such is the Bodhisattva ideal of the Mahayana, a man who is done with self, whose head and heart are given for all time to the service of mankind, and who is content to stand aside and wait for his own reward 'until the last blade of grass is entered into Buddhahood'.

The light grows. There comes the moment of conversion, the 'turning about at the seat of consciousness' which is the beginning of the journey home. By one path or another we approach the entrance to the final path which is the same for all. It leads from illusion to awareness of the truth within, from self to No-self, to the Beyond of difference. Now we must teach, with doctrine possibly, but more by what we are. It has been nobly said that 'no man can more greatly help his brother than by the spectacle of his own achieved holiness'. Thus did the Buddha teach. It was because the Buddha was *buddha*, Awakened, that the great minds of the day came to him to kneel and hear.

Let us climb higher. Let us become God, or if you do not like

[1] *The Voice of the Silence.*

the term, become Dharmakaya, the very body of the Law. Let us achieve and be the Buddha within. Let us consider why God created the universe. He did so that he might know himself as God, that he might say, 'Be still, and know that I am God'. He could not say this save to someone, something that was *not* God. Therefore he had to limit himself to know what he was and is and ever more will be, absolute. The Unborn must be born into Samsara without ceasing to be the Unborn. Here is the mystery of incarnation: the descent of spirit into matter, the Fall, the sacrifice. God must sacrifice himself to be God. You and I must sacrifice our 'self' if we would know and become what we are. We must give if we would have, give all if we would have all, and what we give is a pleasure to give, or should be, for it is the not-Self, the illusion that I am I which blinds us from the light of our own enlightenment. 'Forgoing self the universe grows I.'

These are not metaphysics for the fun of it. They have a daily and practical use. Bear with me. Dr Suzuki has written of what he calls Zen logic, by which we see that A is A *because* A is not-A. In his own words, 'The way to approach Buddhahood or enlightenment is to concretize the logic, 'A' is 'A' because 'A' is 'Not-A' in your own experience. This is to understand the un-understandable.' It is indeed important to understand that A is A *because* A is not-A, that all is as it is *because* it is not. This must be so, because within everything is the essential 'is-ness' of that thing. A is A because of the essential A-ness of A. Could it be otherwise? And the A-ness of A and the B-ness of B likewise and equally are not-A, not-B, that is, No-mind, No-thing, the absolute. What is the A-ness of A, the suchness which makes it A? It is the suchness that makes B, B, the oakness of the oak, the watchness of my watch on the table. Each in itself is utterly, irrevocably and precisely 'just so' and not otherwise. The form eternally changes but each thing is what it is by reason of what it is not, its suchness which is, but is not. It is, I repeat 'just so'. And the suchness which makes it just so is its Non-duality.

But this is God's view, which sees no difference between any two things, no difference whatsoever. This is a state of awareness before duality was born, that sees in each changing form only the 'Essence of pure mind', as Hui-neng called it, the 'nothing between', the essential suchness of the Void. How then shall we stay with God's view, with the Buddha's all-seeing eye, now that in a fleeting concept we have at least imagined the final negative of the Void? I have a suggestion to make. It has been said that a man believes a doctrine when he behaves as if it were true. Let us live, then, 'as if'. For if it be true, why not live in the truth of it? What hinders? Only I. But if I begin here and now to live as if what is true is actually true, shall I not grow nearer to the truth I live? Let us try, looking to the suchness of things in all things, and beginning to see that there is no difference between them save in the accidents of the changing form. This is at least a beginning. Will it not lead to quietude of heart and mind, to greater serenity? As we move to the centre, where the spinning wheel of unreal living dies to stillness, we shall surely find that 'It's all right'. That every thing is as it should be, just so, the result of past causes, the working out of the vast cycles of becoming which form our universe. In our personal lives we shall stop pushing, whether our views, our desires, our personalities. We shall be content to be pushed around, feeling ourselves as 'nothing special', and in rare moments as nothing at all!

Is all this living a lie, because we are not enlightened? No, because we are! We are merely acting 'as if' the temporary screen of self had been removed, and we saw no longer as in a glass, darkly, but directly, into the suchness of all things and the No-self, No-mind which lies 'beyond'.

This means living in two worlds at once, but we already do so. We live in the light, but parts of us function in the darkness of illusion, of selfish foolish desire. But as we learn to see all things, each situation, everybody as 'just so', the light of our inherent suchness, more and more of the light will illumine the person who goes to the office, who works in the home. Living, as if we are what we are, we shall be nearer to the ultimate ideal, 'to live life as it lives itself', and to seek no further.

I close with a quotation from Chuang Tzu used by Dr Suzuki in a recent monograph. 'The wise man knows how to make use of the principle of Identity through the maze of contrary ideas . . . he surrenders himself to that which transcends all individual differences . . . He has no cravings for anything else. He rests with himself *now*.' Just so.

25

Zen Comes West

Western Buddhism stands at the cross-roads. In popular parlance it has reached the point of no-return. It has moved far from being one of a hundred alien and peculiar beliefs studied by a few enthusiasts, and become an integral part of Western thought. Some of its schools are well established. Theravada study and practice is to be found in many of the European countries, the Prajnaparamita philosophy is being taken up under the lectures and writings of Dr Edward Conze, Tibetan ritual is active in parts of Europe, and now Zen has become so popular that it is in danger of becoming a cult.

From such a position it must needs go forward; the movement is now too deeply rooted to wither from want of attention or be killed by its inevitable foes. 'Western Buddhism' has passed from the condition of an idle phrase, and is becoming a visible fact. Whether there should be such a thing is beside the point; it is born and it is growing, and it means that the Buddhism of Europe will not be the Buddhism of Ceylon, or of China or Tibet, which are very different in form; nor will its Zen be entirely the Zen Buddhism of Japan.

But the Buddhism of the West will be still more different from that of the East than those of Ceylon and Tibet, for example, are from each other. The Eastern approach to Truth is, as Lily Abegg proves in *The Mind of East Asia*, total and intuitive; that of the West is analytic/synthetic and mainly intellectual. Its starting point is the vaunted 'scientific' approach to phenomena, whether objective or in the mind. It moves from the particular to the general, from visible material to intellectual hypotheses; it believes in believing nothing until you must. It follows that a definitely Western Buddhism must in time emerge, and be none the less Buddhism for being Western. The same applies to Zen. The aim of Zen Buddhism is the direct approach to Non-duality, and nothing less. All else is secondary, including morality, doctrine, and every kind of ritual. Zen Buddhism was born in China of Bodhidharma and Tao, with Indian Buddhism as its reincarnating 'source material'. It passed to Japan, and is now associated with the culture which it built among that highly cultured people. Now the Japanese offer the West its history, its theory and doctrine, its practice in monasteries and in daily life, and its records of achievement.

These we import through the books of Dr. D. T. Suzuki, whose name is all but coterminous with Zen as known and practised in the West. But we shall not import these goods and leave them permanently foreign, as Chinese restaurants, French fashions and American films. Rather we shall receive them, study them, test them, digest them, absorb their spirit and then reclothe them in our own idiom of thought and practice. Only in this way will they become the product and expression of our own minds, and thus a useful set of 'devices' to enable us to find and express 'our' Zen, that is, Zen as we shall find it.

Or shall we lose the thing we want in making Western clothes for it? Will Zen in the West be so intellectualized, not only in the approach to it, but the thing when found, that it may be splendid but will not be Zen. The answer will depend on our power to achieve it for what it is, if not by Japanese technique then by something more appropriate, though we shall not lightly discard a method which has served the millions of the East for fifteen hundred years. It is true that Carl Jung and others have stressed the folly of the West attempting to import the spiritual technique of the East by the process of intellectual adoption, for in this way it is not grafted on to the individual unconscious so as to present a vital and natural growth. But as the great writer points out in the same volume,[1] in spiritual affairs 'everything depends on the man and little or nothing on the method', which is only 'the way laid down by the man that his action may be

[1] *The Secret of the Golden Flower*, p. 97.

the true expression of his nature'. If some in the West, therefore, find the Japanese technique a way which aptly expresses their own search for Reality, let them use it. Those dissatisfied can seek or create their own.

Meanwhile the Eastern and Western approach to the same goal is different, and the difference is well set out in two books on Zen,[1] the one by Dr Suzuki and the other by Alan Watts. But it is not fair to take Dr Suzuki's books as a sample of Eastern writing on Zen. He is unique and likely to remain so. There are other scholar-philosophers with a knowledge of Zen Buddhism; there are Roshis in Japan who, writing nothing, have yet achieved a first-hand experience of Reality. Is there any other who, with the training of a philosopher, with enormous knowledge of Buddhism in Japanese, Chinese, Sanskrit and Pali, and a knowledge of Western thought in several languages, can yet say, with all the unclaimed authority of one who knows, what is Reality? For forty years, from *Essays in Zen Buddhism, Series I*, in 1927, he has spoken to the world, both East and West, as far as any man in modern times has done so, from the plane of Prajna. Only from him can we take the logic of No-logic, and see that A is at the same time Not-A. He truly is a living bridge from the Absolute to the Relative, a leader from the Unreal to the Real that dwells in the Unreal, and those still locked in the cage of concept, who cannot see him so, are to be pitied for their chains.

Who else presents the Japanese way of Zen? Professor Sohaku Ogata wrote a brief work on *Zen for the West* on the strength of two years' work in the USA and three months in Europe. But for him Dr Suzuki is the Master, one whose very presence takes one further on the way, and he would not claim to stand beside him. Yet, these Eastern teachers alike criticize the West for being too intellectual. Herrigel alone, they seem to say, in his *Zen in the Art of Archery* has caught the spirit of Zen, but then he learnt it from a Master of Zen in Japan. This rules out my own *Zen Buddhism*, Benoit's *The Supreme Doctrine*, and Robert Linssen's *The Living Zen*. It also rules out Alan Watts' *Spirit of Zen* and his later work, his *magnum opus* on the subject, *The Way of Zen*. Can nobody, then, write usefully on Zen who has

[1] *Mysticism, Christian and Buddhist*, Allen and Unwin, 13s 6d.
The Way of Zen, Thames and Hudson, 25s.

not studied long in a Zen monastery? No words can express the discovery of Zen, but even a Japanese *Roshi* uses them, and if the West is more thoughtfully than intuitively inclined we must find a technique which begins with thought and then by finer and finer thought transcends it. Clearly the intuition is needed to achieve Prajna, and Western minds are paralyzed by a system of education which does not recognize its existence. Very well, then, we must examine and develop this faculty of direct cognition, and then use it to attain what thought can never know. How? If we cannot borrow teachers from Japan to help us until we produce our own, can we fight our way through the darkness until the most mystically minded among us not only find the Way but are able to teach it to others?

For the East has no monopoly of *satori*, and though *satori* is one, it may be expressed by those who achieve it in different ways, according to temperament. Professor Ogata told us of those who react with a tremendous feeling of gratitude; these are the devotional or *tariki* type. Others are filled with overwhelming joy; these are the self-reliant, thinking type of *jiriki*. But, I asked him, why not a third, the Karma-yogins of Indian philosophy, if the previous two equate with Bhakti and Jnana Yoga? We in the West love action: action is our criterion of right. An act is 'good form', or 'it isn't done', and in any thought or situation we ask 'How does it work out?' or, 'What shall I do about it?' Would this third reaction be the worse for being new? This assumes, of course, that we attain *satori*, but the type-reaction to it may indicate the divers ways by which it may be approached. And if we in the West are Karma-yogins, seeking the Real by right action, it may be there is a way of right action by which to attain and then to express our *satori*.

Perhaps the Western approach should be: A groundwork of the basic principles of Buddhism and Buddhist thought. The development of a well-balanced mind that can concentrate, can analyze the ingredients of Zen so far as they are subject to analysis, and then build a synthesis. Then meditation, to soften the limitations of thought, to develop the intuition towards the inter-diffusion of opposites, and progressively to illumine thought with the light of intuitive awareness. We shall not be alone in the latter and all-important phase. Eckhart led the way as a Christian mystic; and astronomers and physicists of today are alike discovering that matter is but motion visible, and that all matter might be described as thought within a Cosmic Mind. As this Mind is found to be one All-mind, the possibility of No-thought as the goal of thought, and the awareness of thought as the screen which hides Reality from us will become a certainty. Flashes of the indescribable Non-dual will come, and at once be destroyed by attempts to rationalize them. Then they will be accepted for what they are, moments of super-intellectual awareness of a Light above the darkness of mere thought. Then more and longer flashes; then Zen 'moments' achieved by deliberate exercise of meditation, backed by a trained and indomitable will. When this is integrated into a system of approach to Zen, will it not stand comparison, as a new development from the Western mystical tradition, with the sporadic experience of what my colleagues have irreverently described as *koan*-busters? Perhaps not; in which case I will take my thirty blows as a man.

Let us look, then, at Dr Suzuki's noble work, and see what is here that a Western mind, fighting to pass beyond its own limitations, cannot with will and imagination suddenly and memorably 'see'.

In the very first chapter of *Mysticism, Christian and Buddhist,* Dr Suzuki sets out what he has long disclosed in many of his works, his enthusiastic adoption of Eckhart as not only the greatest of Western mystics but one who in his own terminology was talking Zen. He quotes Ananda Coomaraswamy, a fellow enthusiast, on Eckhart's 'astonishingly close parallel to Indian modes of thought', not by borrowing but because of 'the coherence of the metaphysical tradition in the world at all times'. Eckhart knew the distinction of Godhead from God, of the indescribable Absolute and its first manifestations. He even described, as Dr Suzuki frequently describes, why God created the Universe, that He might know Himself. If Eckhart, a German, can so find, cannot we too? True, Eckhart left no pupils, but then Zen Buddhism is unique in this, that it is the sole school in which such mystical experience is not only taught, but the way to it is taught, and pupils are trained in turn to teach.

And Buddhist philosophy is again unique in that it is based

on the Buddha's personal experience. 'Whatever knowledge the philosopher must have, it must come out of his experience,' which is 'seeing', seeing things in their state of suchness or 'isness', a term which Eckhart himself employs. In brief, 'personal experience is the foundation of Buddhist philosophy, and the function of the intellect consists in leading the mind to a higher field of consciousness by proposing questions which are beyond itself'. Thus we in the West must go on asking until we learn that the intellect alone will not answer. For 'Zen's first concern is about its experience and not its modes of expression'. These are of the field of action in which the West excels, yet so in a way is experience, for *satori* is not an abstract idea but a concrete fact, as lightning is a concrete fact.

What 'self' acquires it? St Paul spoke of body, soul and spirit. We know the body, and soul and spirit are fundamentally two, though one. And Dr Suzuki, in a single paragraph, sweeps aside the tedium of the Theravada's views on self, re-unites the Dharma with the Indian source from which it emerged, and raises the eyes of the individual part to the Whole which is infinite. After speaking of the *gahakarika*, the 'builder of the house' of self from which, being free, the newly enlightened one knows that he is free, he says: 'The *gahakarika* is our relative, empirical ego, and the mind freed from its binding conditions (*sankhara*) is the absolute ego, Atman, as it is elucidated in the Nirvana Sutra. The denial of Atman as maintained by earlier Buddhists refers to Atman as the relative ego and not to the absolute ego, the ego after enlightenment-experience. Enlightenment is seeing the absolute ego as reflected in the relative ego and acting through it' (p. 47). Here is the world of our own experience, of a better and worse self, of the one that must be slain that the other may know itself as it is, 'self-identified' or 'inter-diffused' with the Absolute.

There is nothing here to negative my thesis, that though the early stages on the journey may be harder for Westerners than for their Eastern brothers on the Way, it is one way to one end, to be found not in a heaven which is elsewhere, but in the 'one moment' which is here and now and doing this. How then, does Alan Watts' new book assist his fellow-Westerners to achieve the same 'experience'? He does not claim to have studied in

Japan, nor to have had any training under a Roshi in the USA, but he still has the brilliant mind which gave us *The Spirit of Zen* at the age of nineteen, and he has learnt enough Chinese to read originals for himself.

With this equipment, being dissatisfied with any existing book on the subject, in that none gives what is to him essential, the Taoist and Indian background, he sets out to supply the deficiency. In his Preface he says, 'I am not in favour of "importing" Zen from the Far East, for it has become deeply involved with cultural institutions which are foreign to us. But there are things which we can learn, or unlearn, from it and apply in our own way.' So far we agree, but I do not see the need for his suggested third position between the 'objective' observer of Zen who, as he brightly points out, eats the menu instead of the dinner, and the 'subjective' disciple who does not know what dinner is being eaten. As he himself says, 'To know what Zen is, and especially what it is not, there is no alternative but to practise it, to experiment with it in the concrete so as to discover the meaning which underlies the words'. But this can only be done from 'inside' with the full enthusiasm of a mind bent to that end. When he wishes to add some measure of the objective Western viewpoint I am with him, and would refer to the second step of my own suggested Western approach to Zen, but there is no need for the 'friendly neutral position' he proposes. (As the Master Ummon said, 'If you walk just walk. If you sit, just sit. But don't wobble.') There need be no fear of our entanglement in the 'institutions' of Zen Buddhism, unless the fear is of becoming impaled on the finger instead of looking at the moon. But if the West, in its practice of Zen, is prepared to create its own institutions the trouble will not arise.

And so he gives us a most admirable book which, even if it is, as Professor Ogata said in his long review of it, 'an artist's creation of a big cat in an attempt to draw a tiger', is yet for many of us a large and helpful cat. He tells us of the philosophy of Tao, of the rise of Buddhism and the development of the Mahayana (can no two people agree on the cause of this?) and then sets out 'The Rise and Development of Zen'. Here, in a series of brief sketches of the Patriarchs, from Bodhidharma to Hui-neng, he imperceptibly prepares us for the second part of the book, on 'Principles and Practice'. He extracts and describes with ample illustration what to him are the factors in Zen Buddhism which make it unique; its directness, its naturalness, its having 'nothing special' to say or do, its 'going ahead without hesitation' (so admirably shown in the daily life of Professor Ogata), its purposelessness and its exquisite simplicity. In brief, an excellent book for the Western student. It does not give him Zen; nor does any other book, but it may set his feet on the Way which leads to it.

To sum up—if I can—my yet uncertain thoughts on a vast and urgent subject, the West needs Zen and Japan has it. But the West must have Zen without its Japanese clothing as soon as Western clothing can be made for it. But the clothing is unimportant compared with the achievement of the experience. How to attain the experience without a visit to Japan? The answer is—by study of the background of Buddhism and the history of Zen, by meditation, regular and deep, by the deliberate cultivation, by all 'devices' possible, of the power of the intuition, and by having in Europe from time to time such help from Japan as we need, until our own Roshis have emerged and been given the 'seal of transmission', that they in turn may train their pupils to that same high office and responsibility.

26

Buddhism Comes West

'There is nothing, or almost nothing, in the Buddhist interpretation of spiritual truth which ties it to any soil or any climate, to any race or tribe. . . . In Buddhism there is nothing which cannot be easily transported from one part of the world to another.' Thus Dr Conze, in his excellent *Buddhism*, and the history of Buddhism proves him to be right. Buddhism has arrived in Europe, not merely as the study of the dilletante few but as a growing factor in the aggregate Western mind. What is this Buddhism? Is it of the Theravada School, or of the Mahayana, or Zen, or a little of all, or a definitely Western form of Buddhism?

Buddhism has always been deeply affected by the religious beliefs of the people to whom it is introduced. One has only to remember the effect on the 'new' religion of the indigenous *nat*-worship of Burma, or the Bön practices of Tibet, or the Taoist-Confucian background in China, to see the reaction of the Dhamma's tolerance of other beliefs on its own external practices, and even on the principles taught in its name. In the same way, the Buddhism of England, and it is of England that I speak with most experience, could never, from the moment it became a living force in the English mind, remain the Buddhism of Ceylon or the Buddhism of China. For the principle of *anicca*, constant change, applies to religions as to all else, and though the life is the life of the Dhamma, the form must vary with the needs of the people who adopt the Buddhist Way.

There is thus in the process of growth, whether one approves of it or not, an English form of Buddhism, which, from the accidents of Western religious history, emphasizes a number of principles which are in the East so taken for granted as to need no mentioning. Where, for example, does one find in the Pali canon an exposition of the principles of karma and rebirth, or stress laid on the fundamental unity of life? Yet these, in the present decay of Christian principles, are truths no longer taught in the West. Here man is believed to be born with his body and to leave this earth for ever when it dies, the length of his life and its fortunes being at the mercy of a vaguely described, omnipotent, but strangely unmerciful God.

Yet until these cardinal principles of the Buddha-Dhamma are restored to the Western mind, it is little use to speak of the Noble Truths, or even of the Eightfold Path. When life is viewed as a brief, uncertain span between the unknown and the unknown, and when all its causes and effects are alike relatable only to an unknown yet personified Cause, of what avail to speak of a Noble Path which through a thousand lives leads man, the pilgrim, to a Goal which is the guerdon of untiring effort under the reign of law?

As a matter of history karma and rebirth and the oneness of life were widely taught in the West before the arrival of Buddhism. They are bodied forth in the works of H. P. Blavatsky, and the Theosophical Society has untiringly proclaimed them throughout the length and breadth of Europe for over eighty years. H. P. Blavatsky and Colonel Olcott, who themselves took Pansil publicly in Ceylon in 1880, were the true pioneers of Western Buddhism, and the part which Theosophy, a modern presentation of the Wisdom that is older than all religions, has played in preparing the Western mind for Buddhism, should not be overlooked.

Nor are *anicca, dukkha, anatta*, the 'three Signs of Being', known only to the West through Buddhism. The doctrine of change has long been known to Europe, and Science accepts it in the laboratory. *Dukkha*, the presence of suffering in all that lives, is a fact which Western philosophers and poets have long attempted to explain, and as for the doctrine of *anatta*, the Western philosopher Hume could discover no self 'other than a bundle or collection of different perceptions which succeed each other with an inconceivable rapidity, and are in a perpetual flux and movement'. Even causation, and the slow evolution of the whole by causal factors, is no new doctrine in the West, though the Wheel of Causation as such is a concept at present far too sweeping for the Western mind.

Experience shows that Buddhism, presented as a series of negatives, will never appeal to the West. For the force which drives man onward to his own salvation is positive, and to be told that there exists no God to save his soul, and no soul to be saved, will help him little if at all. That the Buddhist view of Reality is utterly different from the Western equivalent must be taught in positive terms, by enormously enlarging the concept of 'God'; while, to tell the student that he has no 'soul', i.e. no Self or even self of any kind, is to make a statement which has no Scriptural support and is obviously untrue. In considering the nature of the 'soul' or individual self, however, the Buddhist can enormously assist his Western brother by the Buddhist analysis of self and its parts and faculties, and contribute, in terms acceptable to the Western mind, material for the new-found science of psychology.

What, then, is the form of Western Buddhism? The answer is that it has no rigid form, and it will cease to be useful to the West on the day that it acquires one. As seeds in the wind, so will the principles of the Buddha-Dhamma be offered to the Western mind, to bear fruit, little or a hundredfold, according to the individual mind wherein they find a resting-place. When a builder chooses stone for a building he takes no heed of the mason's name which is marked thereon, save as he comes to associate a certain name with a stone well-formed and of good material. So will the builders of new Europe use those principles which serve their purpose best, and without acknowledgement. The West needs Buddhism, not persons labelled as Buddhists, and Buddhism is the Buddha-Dhamma in any name or none.

This is not to say that the only Buddhism acceptable to the West will be a medley of principles collected and arranged for European consumption. Such a deliberate conflation exists in the 'Twelve Principles of Buddhism' compiled by the Buddhist Society, and now available in sixteen languages. But although such a list is a useful summary for the enquirer, and of even greater use in suggesting the ground which is common to all schools of Buddhism, it is not thus that Buddhism will grow in Europe. On the contrary, history is repeating itself in that when the Buddhism of China reached Japan it did so in a series of schools of Buddhist philosophy which, reaching the younger civilization one after another, each took root in its new surroundings and developed tolerantly side by side with those already arrived. Not until the adoption in 1946 of the Society's Twelve Principles by all the major sects of Japan did there exist even on paper anything which could be described as Japanese Buddhism. In the same way the teachings of the Theravada School, then knowledge of Zen, then knowledge of Tibetan Buddhism, the Prajna-paramita philosophy and the Shin School, arrived from the East *seriatim*, and groups to study all of them exist in a healthy or moribund condition in our midst today. Only in recent years have a number of men and women entered the Buddhist field who, denying allegiance to any one school, prefer to study the whole field for themselves, thereafter specialising or not as their study and practice demand.

Meanwhile, it seems that there is a need for a moral philosophy or way of life to replace the dying hold of Christian dogma on the Western mind. This new technique of living, for such it is, must fulfil at least three needs.

It must in the first place vastly expand the current conception of the Whole. At the moment, time for the individual still begins at birth and dies with the body's death. God is a force, abstract or personified according to the thinker's own development, but painfully limited in form and scope. Western mysticism, too long suppressed, could with advantage be revived and with it the comprehension of the Universe as an infinite and boundless Whole whose essential nature no man can describe, nor even yet conceive. The Brahmins call it THAT; the West could find yet a new name or regard it as the Namelessness. The period of incarnation, and therefore of time for growth must be stretched by a deep understanding of the laws of karma and rebirth, lost to the West since the days of Origen; and men must learn to regard this life on earth as one of a series which springs from a distant past and will only end in a hardly-earned and self-attained perfection. True dignity and self-reliance, basic virtues which began to fade when prayers were first addressed to an extra-Cosmic God, must be restored by expanding the scope of the laws of cause-effect, and there will be time enough to consider with fine precision the nature of the 'Self' that moves from life to life when the pilgrim, on his own unaided feet, has learnt to move. Above all, the conception of the mind must be raised to include that avenue of pure perception, the intuition; for the day of the intellect as the final arbiter of Truth is ended, and the fetters of rational thought must be gradually unloosed.

Secondly, this new 'religion', new only because it will advance just so much on the old, must accord with the findings of Science, using that term to include not merely the results of laboratory search, but also the truly metaphysical re-discoveries of the nature of thought and matter, and the nature and powers of the human mind as expounded in modern psychology.

Thirdly, the West has need of a simple, reasonable way of life which will restore to youth its failing sense of morality, yet need no services or priests to give it form and cogency. Mind, heart and hand must all be harnessed, for belief and devotion to a leader are feeble possessions until they are manifest in action.

To what extent and with what principles can Buddhism fulfil these needs? It is easier to answer the latter than the former question. The principles may be briefly catalogued. The West is increasingly finding what it needs in Karma and Rebirth; in the Oneness of Life, which is the basis of all compassion; in the principles and practice of Zen; in the Mahayana teaching of the Essence of Mind and in the Theravada teaching of the Middle Way as a practical, reasonable, all-embracing and, above all, tested way of life, whereon the pilgrim, ever 'working out his own salvation with diligence', moves from confinement to freedom, from the less to the more, from illusion seen as such to at least a greater Reality.

With karma and rebirth and the oneness of life the West is already, thanks to Theosophy, partly familiar. Zen, the Chinese *ch'an* from the Sanskrit *Dhyana*, is beyond all 'isms', yet the Buddha's Enlightenment is the seed from which it sprang. It begins where the intellect leaves off, and forms an international technique for intuitive and, therefore, direct 'seeing into one's own nature'. Widely studied and hourly used in Western countries, it would restore that impish, irrational heart's illumining which flared up in the Middle Ages of Europe, only to be crushed by the birth of Science and the triumph of the rational mind. The spread of Zen would foster and revive the mysticism all but smothered in the fumes of our factory chimneys, and bring the immediate vision of Truth itself into our midst again.

'The Essence of Mind is intrinsically pure,' wrote the patriarch Hui-neng, and the Mahayana doctrines of the subjective basis of action and the dominant position of Mind in the cosmic-human scheme of things would be of immense advantage in developing Western psychology, and march with the latest discoveries of our scientists in their search for the ultimate basis of matter and its true relation to the mind. As the powers of the mind are unfolded by doctors, psychologists, philosophers, healers and thinkers of every kind, the teaching of the East, where the nature of Mind and its manifold functioning has long been explored, will be of the utmost help.

Man is a religious animal, and a people that has no spiritual faith is a people sad indeed. Christianity, the product of the Church which has substituted an ethical code and a worn-out ritual for the sunlit river of life, no longer feeds the people's hunger for practical guidance and advice on the treading of the daily round. The Eightfold Path awaits them, and is magnificently suited to the Western mind. Whether in its beginning, as right theories, capable of proof by self-experience, or as right ethics, which the youth of today only knows as a series of cold and unpopular commands, or as mind-development, which in a thousand ways is beginning to be viewed as the basis of all future progress, the West has need of this ancient Way which leads 'from desire to peace'. These seeds, which the few have sown in the first half of the century, are ripe for flowering. Already, Buddhism as a force in the shaping of Western thought is greater perhaps than its promoters realize or its foes would care to admit. The principles so taught may in time create a 'Nava-Yana', as Captain Ellam called it, which will in fact be a Western Buddhism. The Western mind may increasingly select what it needs from the doctrines offered, and build them, modified by current ways of thinking, into the shrine of its own ideals. With this each Western Buddhist will be well content, for it was never his purpose to proselytize in the sense of striving to convert. 'Go ye, O Bhikkhus,' was the Buddha's mandate to his followers, 'and wander forth for the gain of the many, for the welfare of the many, in compassion for the world. Proclaim the doctrines glorious, preach ye a life of holiness, perfect and pure.' It is enough for Western Buddhism to see that in the clamour of our restless and unhappy age the Lion's Roar of Truth is not forgotten, and that the message of the Blessed One, which, in the turning of the wheel of time has lightened the Way to countless of our fellow-men, should be made available to Western minds as they have need of it.

These principles, then, will increasingly supply our Western spiritual needs. Will they, as 'Buddhism', replace the hundred other 'isms' in which at present men believe? At least it has no fear of them.

Alone among the great 'religions' it has no fear of science. Year by year the truths of Buddhism are found by science to be true; none has been disproved. Nor is it fearful of psychology, for the intricate and profound analysis of consciousness to be found in the *Abhidhamma* has yet to be rivalled by western psychology. Social science, one of the youngest gods of modern thought, is a god-child of the Bodhisattva doctrine of supreme compassion for all forms of life, and the duty of each unit of that life to work for the welfare of his fellow men. Of the relation between Buddhism and Christianity nothing useful can be said, for the individual who needs a Way must study all and choose his own. Large numbers of Christian-educated men and women join the Buddhist Society; their reason is their own affair and none would ask them for it.

Will Buddhism, then, replace the reigning gods of Europe? Certainly not. The Western mind is far too virile to adopt the second-hand clothing of another age, and Buddhism as such will never become the religion of England, nor, for that matter, the Way of Life of most of its inhabitants. More and more will the leading minds of the day be attracted to its teaching, but always the many will look for something which the Dhamma will not give. There is in the Theravada School no word of vicarious salvation or atonement, no Saviour to stand between the individual and the consequences, good or evil, of his deeds. Here are no services, no prayer, no mass hysteria on a large or trifling scale wherein the emotions are given the outlet which, in a people emotionally starved and repressed, it is possible they need.

It is true that, in the Mahayana, practices have developed which tend to bridge the gap between religions as such and the Buddha-Dhamma, and there are schools of ritual and of devotion which might provide, if they ever took root in the West, the food which this religious type of mind demands. These practices, however, are not of the essence of Buddhism, and those who feel the need of ritual and the other factors of the religious life can probably find what they want elsewhere. It will certainly be a sad day in the history of Western Buddhism when the Dharma of the All-Enlightened One is debased, in any way whatever, to suit the needs of those unwilling to tread the Buddha's Way to a state of mind beyond the need for all such practices.

27

World Buddhism

Buddhism is a word derived from the Sanskrit *buddh*, that awakening or enlightenment which made an Indian princeling assume the title of Buddha, and indeed, Sambuddha, the fully Enlightened One. Buddhism, a Western term for the vast corpus of thought which has grown about his name and title, has been defined as 'a rationalization of the Buddha's spiritual experience'. Certainly his Dhamma was his attempt to show all men the Way to the supreme experience which had been achieved by one man, himself. What happened to that Message?

To answer this question we must glance again at Buddhist history and geography. In India itself, the Teaching was soon developed into divers schools, of which the oldest to survive is one of the eighteen forms of the Hinayana, now known as the Theravada. This form settled in south and south-east Asia, and today is that of Ceylon, Thailand, Burma and Cambodia.

The Mahayana, based on the magnificent Prajna-paramita thought of some of the greatest minds produced in India, itself split into many forms, and spread in the course of centuries North and East into Tibet and Mongolia, China, Korea and Japan. The point to be noted is that every nation and culture, as it received the Message, adopted and adapted it, school by school, in each case adding new schools, or a blend of several, on its own.

By about A.D. 1200 the position was much as we find it today. The Theravada, which had remained comparatively static from the time of Buddhaghosa, was complete with its Pali canon. Tibetan Buddhism had settled into its curious composite form, with four main schools or traditions based on Theravada principles, with Mahayana doctrines superimposed, and grafted onto these the modified Tantras of Bengal.

China accepted many of the schools as they arrived from the West, and produced several of its own, notably Ch'an Buddhism, which is better known today by its Japanese name of Zen. Japan accepted all the Chinese schools as they were brought to the country, extended the Jodo School into its own developed form of Shin, and produced its own Nichiren sect.

Basic Principles

Thus the process in time and space was one of decentralization, fragmentation, specialization, and the appearance of wide variation in doctrine and ritual. But all these schools—as any student may verify for himself—have at heart a body of basic principles common to all. Some twenty years ago I tried to formulate them in 'Twelve Principles of Buddhism', which, translated into sixteen languages, have been accepted by Buddhist authorities in various parts of the Buddhist world.

Now, what had each of these Buddhist schools to do with politics? The answer of course, depends on the definition given to 'politics', but it must include the theory and practice of national government. But is there any large-scale movement affecting the minds and hearts of the community which has not some effect upon that nation's government? To take any part whatsoever in the public affairs of the country is to enter politics; equally, to abstain from all participation, as a formulated policy, is itself, as we have learnt in the last fifty years, a powerful form of politics, for it has direct affect on the minds of those who govern, as on those who elect those governors to power.

The concern with politics by Buddhist schools of thought has, of course, varied with the nation concerned. Generally speaking, until recently the Sangha of the Theravada has abstained from interference in public affairs. On the other hand, the temporal and spiritual government of Tibet was, until the Chinese invasion, in the hands of the same body of men, led by one in whom both powers were manifest. In the middle ages in Japan the monks of certain monasteries took violent part in political affairs;

since 1868, they have taken no part, until the recent phenomenon of new 'religions', one of which, the Soka Gakkai, proclaims
itself a Buddhist group which frankly aims at supreme political
power.

Let us look for a moment at the history of co-operation among
Buddhist nations and sects at a level short of politics. The out-
standing historical event was the foundation and long life of the
Buddhist University of Nalanda, in North-east India, which
flourished from the second to the eleventh centuries A.D. Here
every shade of opinion was expressed, all schools made welcome.
Here, it is said, ten thousand students could choose from a
hundred lectures a day by the greatest minds of the time.

But though all schools were welcome, Buddhist nations as
such were not concerned. A thousand years passed before Dr
G. P. Malalasekera founded the World Fellowship of Buddhists,
to the eternal credit of Ceylon. Its Charter expressly forbids participation in politics, a mandate which some, who seem to regard
the Fellowship as a Buddhist UN, find difficult to accept.

What, then, can the Fellowship do? It can, by regular Con-
ferences, slowly replace mutual ignorance and indifference
between Buddhist schools, and hence of Buddhist nations, with
informed co-operation and goodwill. By frequent interchange of
individuals and groups, of laymen and monks, it can foster the
growth of international, super-national Buddhist feeling. By
personal visits, exchange and translation of books, and exchange
of news, it can foster and increase this feeling between Con-
ferences. The news should be fresh and factual, contained in one
or more periodicals, primarily aimed at its collection and distribution.

This is being done to some extent by *World Buddhism*, published in Ceylon, and by the equivalent which issues now from
Bangkok. International periodicals, such as the *Maha Bodhi
Journal*, and *The Middle Way*, both of which penetrate all over
the world, carry news and views in articles which help to remove
intolerance. All this, and the ceaseless correspondence between
individuals, is helping to create the fact of 'World Buddhism',
and tending to make Buddhism a corporate entity as distinct
from the vaguely connected doctrines of many and divers cultures in scattered parts of the world.

All this, however, is not in the first place, meant to affect the actions of any particular government. There is as yet no parallel to the part which Christianity played in Europe in the middle ages, or the Church of Rome in certain countries today. But it must have some effect, and we are foolish to deny it. Collective thought and feeling affects the electors in any land where the citizen has a say in his country's affairs, even where the government claims to be purely secular.

If a well-organized section of the community collectively holds views on any subject, the government of the day is foolish to ignore those views. Thus Buddhist principles, in one guise or another, can affect all those in political control to act in Buddhist ways, of non-violence, tolerance, and the individual's right to 'work out his own salvation, with diligence'.

This, however, is only indirect participation in politics. What of direct action? It is not enough to say that it is inadvisable or even regrettable. Must we not face the fact that it has arrived, and is growing? The heroic self-immolation by members of the Sangha in Vietnam by way of protest against government action stirred public imagination throughout the world, and has no doubt 'proved' for years to come that the Buddhist Sangha in general is a militant organization. The Sangha of Thailand and to a less extent that of Burma is linked with government decrees as in the Established Church in England. In Ceylon there is still contentious argument on the right of the Sangha to interfere in politics, and in Japan we hear of monks in vociferous action on behalf of Communist China.

But surely it is a contradiction in terms to speak of a Buddhist monk concerned in national politics as such? Surely, his very membership of the Order confines him to study, practice and promulgation of the Dhamma, to setting an example of the holy life? Is not his prestige in the eyes of the people measured by his success in this regard? In matters affecting the Sangha as a whole, the government of any Buddhist country would be wise to keep in touch with some Council of the Sangha, but how can any bhikkhus, much less a body of bhikkhus, use violence of argument, much less violence of action, in national affairs?

Yet such is happening. Is it too late to stop it? If unchecked, does not this very action stain the prestige acquired by the

World Fellowship in its patient creation of a collective feeling of goodwill, tolerance and corporate action for the good of all? As national governments the world over become more and more secular, repudiating all responsibility for the religious education of the young, surely Buddhists, presumably led by the Sangha, of each country where the Dhamma is a spiritual force, must see that this force is exercised at spiritual and not martial levels, as an example to mankind of rule by Dhamma, and not by war.

In brief, world Buddhism is becoming a reality and should be encouraged to develop as such with all speed. The World Fellowship is the best and indeed at present, the only medium through which this force can be expressed. We must therefore help it with funds, goodwill, and active help. But we are then collectively responsible for the way in which this international force is used. Must we not condemn the action of Buddhist monks and laymen alike who resort to force to achieve political ends?

Only thus, it seems, will the Fellowship work to raise the level of national as of international politics, and not itself be debased by them. Only thus will the individual Buddhist, who still finds honour in that name, be working to the goal achieved and proclaimed by the All-Enlightened One, to seek and expose the cause of the world's suffering, the selfishness of men and groups of men, and tread himself, strenuous and mindful every hour of the day, that Path which leads to the end of suffering, for himself and all mankind.

28

The Buddhist Way of Life

Buddhism is a way of life, from first to last a matter of experience. For the Way is a way to the supreme experience by which Gautama, the man, became Buddha, the Fully-Awakened One. Buddhism, therefore, though inevitably including a set of doctrines must, if it is to be true to its genesis, be at the same time a matter of doctrine applied. Hinduism, that vague term for a heterogenous collection of Indian teaching, may be largely philosophy; the Buddha's call to all men was to move from the static to the dynamic, to eschew all futile argument on the 'Indeterminates', such as the nature of the First Cause or the final effect, and to move and keep on moving towards his own Enlightenment. For these questions can never be usefully answered. The First Cause is necessarily beyond, because prior to, causation, and that which is out of manifestation is beyond the reach of words. Buddhism has no use for belief, save in the sense that a man believes a doctrine when he behaves as if it were true. Nor has it any place for faith, save in the reasonable description by a Guide of a Path and its Goal. 'Thus have I found,' said that Guide, 'and this is the Way to that discovery. I tell you the steps on the Way, its dangers and difficulties, the fierce resistance offered by the self, the lures to beguile you into some other way which leads still deeper into the mire of suffering.' Meanwhile that the Way is worthy may be proved at every stage. For treading it there are two rules and only two: Begin, and walk on. Once the first step is taken—and where else than here and now?—each further stage will reveal a wider range of view, an air more pure to breathe, more light as the clouds of our present illusion and desire are, not so much dispersed, as quietly plodded through.

The beginning and end of the Dhamma, then, is experience, the Buddha's supreme experience under the Bo-Tree, and yours and mine. All doctrines constellate about it. The Signs of Being show the nature of the world about us which we ourselves created, and in our reaction to which we begin the experience by which, to keep the obvious analogy, we climb. Experience in action is karma, and though its implications are frightening, we must be brave and walk with courage in a world wherein each littlest action is the fruit of a million causes, and our every thought and act the father of a million million effects. If our responsibility grows each hour for all that we think and feel and do, let us live accordingly, with newly controlled, self-conscious, thoughtful lives. And the right use of karma is to apply it to the Four Noble Truths. Is not all in some sense suffering? Is not its cause the illusion of self and the cries of self for self in the darkness of illusion? How then, shall we remove the desire which makes us do the acts which cause the suffering? The answer is by treading the Path patiently and fully revealed as it mounts by a way made visible, if not yet easy, by the feet of those in front of us, to a summit which we shall not 'know' until we reach it. Yet sometimes when the night is at its darkest hour, we experience, as lightning in the mind, a direct and blinding glimpse of that Light which will, when we have made it so, be the common light of day.

Buddhism, then, is the process of learning by experience to approach, by a gradual or a 'sudden' path, the supreme Experience of the All-Enlightened One. The knowledge of the scholar will prepare the mind, the debates of the intellect may clear the way of intellectual fog, but just as we begin to drive a car when it first moves under our wondering and frightened hands, and to move to the journey's end when we put down the map and open the front door, so we begin to attain enlightenment when we—well, when we begin.

Before a man gains anything worth having he must want it, whether it is a job, a house or salvation, and for anything of spiritual value he must want it, as the Zen Master said, as much as a man whose head is held under water wants air. For though unworthy desire must be eliminated, it is foolish to argue that all desire is evil, for if so with what do we strive to attain Enlightenment? What, then, do we want? Pleasure? It is there, if earned. Happiness? Do we know what we mean by the term, and in the last analysis does it rise above material comfort and an absence of responsibility? What, then, do we count more worthy of our desire than these? Salvation? If so of what, from what and by whom? It is important that these questions be answered, for of those who desire salvation few can answer them. The constant demand, though seldom admitted, is for some other Power or Being or Force to save us from the well-earned consequences of our sins and with the minimum effort by the sinner. Yet there are those whose desire aims higher—for Enlightenment.

All great men worthy of the name have this in common, the sheer size or scope of mind. A great man has a great mind, and the image springs to hand of space, of a sunlit grandeur swept by the winds of heaven, and void, utterly void, of our human pettiness, or self. Enlightenment is a pregnant term, and so is awakening, the true meaning of the root word *budh* from which is derived the title *Buddha*, the Awakened One. Herein is no *avidya* left, no mist of uncertainty, no darkness of illusion. These are the marks of self-hood which lives in duality and difference; Enlightenment is the awareness of a Oneness beyond all difference, of a knowledge direct and perfect, so far as this be possible in manifestation, of the Absolute. Is this worth having, or even a foretaste of its unstained serenity?

Then what is the price that the would-be purchaser must pay? There must be immediate deposit of much time and thought and energy. Then dearer belongings must be sacrificed. All our prejudice must go, our dear opinions and entrenched beliefs, whether inherited or later acquired by solemn reasoning, or by chance formation from a first impression, or a neighbour's word. Our present sense of values must be forfeit, and a wiser set developed. For our likes and dislikes are seldom reasonable, and our place on this or the other side of the fence in politics or social life was seldom reasonably acquired. But however formed they will prove a hindrance to the cool, impersonal understanding which is a faculty of the great, because enlightened mind. In the end we must pay the final penalty, our most endeared possession, self itself. How shall a mind be great whose voice at all times cries, and cries but little else than, 'I . . . I . . . I'? Such is the payment, on the instalment system if you will, but yet continuous and painful in the extreme. Yet strangely enough, as payment is perpetually made the purchaser becomes the greater and the richer for the deal. As self and its claims die out, as the dark and cluttered box-room of the mind is expanded into a mighty hall wherein the sunlight and the mountain air sing happily, there will be no regrets for the views and convictions and taught beliefs which, now in the dustbin of the day's meditation, trouble the mind no more.

As the Buddhist pilgrim moves, and makes his sacrifice, his relationship to the Buddha Dhamma will steadily progress. There are, perhaps, four phases on the Way. First, the static: 'I am interested in Buddhism.' Then, when the first step is taken: 'I use it', to be later reversed, at a moment vital to the Pilgrim, and replaced with: 'Now Buddhism uses me'. Finally, the dawn of a joy which has no part with pleasure or happiness as usually conceived: 'I live for the Dhamma and in it, each moment of the day'. Only when the final stage is reached is Bodhicitta born in the heart, the living awareness of the world as one. Then only, when each action is felt to be right because it is the action of the Whole, when the sense of duty and right and the joy of both is fused in a cool serenity, is born the experience of a Way on which no sense of haste, no thought of purpose or reward remains; where the importunity of time is dissolved in a new-found sense of timing, and there is but the next thing to be joyously, impersonally done.

And who decides what is right, and what one's duty? Who but you? There is no God to do it for you, no Authority to tell you what is true, or for that matter what is Buddhism. Study, and deeply, by all means, but while you move. As you move the Way will open, and the answers, all of them, appear.

But there are many obstructions on the Way, fallen tree-trunks, which, once beautiful, are now but a nuisance to all concerned. One is the God-concept which, though it serves its purpose for millions of Westerners, has no place in the Buddhist analysis of life. It may be an admirable conception, this Absolute yet personal Being who, in the intervals of creation of worlds and souls, finds time to assist each pilgrim in his personal affairs, but the Buddhist has no need of it, and finds no evidence to support its existence. Yet the thought is not easily removed from a Western mind. Enlarge it, then. If the Absolute is inconceivable—'The Tao that can be expressed is not the eternal Tao' —dwell on the all-but-inconceivable grandeur of the Absolute. Substitute for the whim of a God the unswerving, living Law of cause-effect, and assume the enormous dignity which grows from awareness that indeed we 'work out our own salvation with diligence'. Then will arise a sense of close companionship with all that lives. Truly the heart is warmed to find that life is one, and all its parts, the noblest and the least, 'members of one another'.

A more serious obstacle in the Buddhist life is the network of illusions which enmesh the Western mind. One is the confusion of thought and emotion in valuing experience. The law of karma, for example, is either true or untrue. If it be true it is irrelevant whether one likes it or not. The same applies to change, or selflessness, or the doctrine of rebirth. Yet a member of an audience will frequently announce, 'I do not like the idea of karma. It sounds cold.' Or, 'I do not wish to come back to earth'. The reply is obvious, that we may not approve the law of gravity as we fall down a well, but the law still operates.

A more subtle error is to believe that the intellect can lead to Truth, whereas it only tells us more and more about it. The intellect deals with concepts, 'things' created by the mind of the substance of thought. Each is composed of a choice of the pairs of opposites, each of which is only partially true. However balanced the new confection of attributes, it is never Truth. The awareness of Truth, which lies in its very nature beyond all reasoning, is achieved by the faculty of *buddhi*, the intuition. This experience, though absolute for the experiencer is unprovable, and indeed indescribable to another. The intellect, though a magnificent instrument, must be developed in order to transcend itself. Not until the light of *buddhi* floods the field of thought is the drear dichotomy of subject-object fused in the new awareness, the direct experience of Reality.

The third and last illusion is self. Only when self is analyzed, and the student finds for himself that none of its parts is permanent, will this chattering monkey of self be quietened and in the end dissolved. Then the mind, in increasing harmony with All-Mind—and the nature of this is a matter of experience—knows itself as one with the universe, and an instrument in the evolution of the Whole. Wisdom-Compassion are found to be twin forces for the using, not for possession, and as room is made for them in place of self, the size and strength of these forces in the mind increase accordingly. Truly the great man is a power for good, for he offers less and less resistance to the light which, when it shines in any mind, is the light of Enlightenment.

With a lessening of illusion, and the growth of Mind in mind, what a swift improvement is made in controlled reactions to the day's environment? Karma itself is found to be the most exciting of the new thoughts in the mind. Meditate but an hour on the fact that there is no luck, no chance, no fate and no coincidence in life. Then face the reverse. All things flow from a preceding cause; all things have an effect on all. One's lightest thought or emotion or act has effect, on one plane or another, on all in the room, in the town, in the world, in the universe; and the littlest act of all in the country, on the earth, in the universe is affecting you. What new responsibility is here, and what complete removal of our favourite pass-time, complaint? For why complain when you are to blame, you and your brothers-in-One?

The 'Signs of Being', when applied, can change our view of life profoundly. All must agree on the law of change, but how many live as though it were true? Is increasing age accepted or resisted; do we regard our possessions as held in trust for all, or as things which we have successfully attached to 'me', and the removal of which, from any cause, we deeply resent? There is no self, but we all fear death. Why, when it is inevitable from the moment of birth and in fact each life's supreme experience? We agree that we move unceasingly to something different, yet we insure ourselves so that so far as possible nothing about ourselves shall change. Ever we fear to lose our jobs or homes or children; seldom are we content to let slip our self-made moorings and to move unfettered, anchorless, upon the stream of experience down to the Shining Sea. As for suffering, who doubts that it pertains to all our being, in each moment of the day? Do we accept it as self-wrought, face it, digest it; in brief, experience it; or do we resent it and strive to escape, into pleasure, unreal thoughts, or death?

'Compassion is no attribute. It is the law of Laws, eternal harmony . . . a shoreless universal essence, the light of everlasting right, and fitness of all things, the law of Love eternal.' Such is the Law—do we live by it? He is a most unusual man who habitually looks on his fellow men as brothers, as pilgrims on the same path to the same far distant Goal, and behaves to them accordingly. Yet if life is one, and the least form of it holy with that life, why is a world that should be learning by the experience ever at war? Because each man is at war within, and not till the war is won for compassion against the powers of hatred, lust, and the illusion of separation in each individual mind will the mass-mind of a nation, or of the few who direct it, truly want what only then they will achieve, peace.

The sweetly reasonable Four Noble Truths are clearly true, that we suffer, and that the cause of our suffering is self. Do we, from dawn to bedtime, strive to remove that cause? Yet the mere analysis of the thing called 'I' will soon work wonders. When temper is lost, who lost control of what? What fears that this and this will happen, and does it matter if it does? These fearsome happenings we fear; if we let them come shall we wake in the morning? We shall. These problems that we fear to face, who made them? We made them, with a combination of reasoning, usually bad reasoning, and emotion, in itself a cause of suffering. Let us walk up to the problem, in full awareness that it does not exist outside our mind! It will not be easy to reach it, for as we approach it moves away, like the morning mist on the road that looks so solid ahead but which, as we move towards it, is never reached. We made the problem and threw it ahead upon the Way. We approach and are frightened by it. Yet if we still walk on it is never there. As Dr Graham Howe said of the precipice ahead of us. 'Some stop at the sight of it; some go round, or try to. Some go back. Why not go on and over?' This is at least most admirable Zen.

Yet the man who applies the truths he has found to be true will soon be faced with a fierce obstruction, albeit it comes from within. The reaction of *tamas,* as the Indian philosophers call it, is evoked and strengthened by the force by which we now walk on. *Tamas,* the force of inertia, darkness, laziness, can speak in many voices, all of them liars of considerable skill. 'Don't overdo it, old chap. Take it easy.' 'Why not wait till next month to begin? You'll have more time then.' 'If you overdo it you'll have a bad setback.' Thus, with that modicum of truth which makes a lie more easily digested, the voice of laziness holds one back upon the Way. And the obstruction is no phantasy, for Western psychology knows of the reaction of the unconscious to the deliberate movements of the conscious mind. And a thing in the mind is as real, in the relative world, as a fallen tree on the road.

How, then, do we travel up the mountain side, in the acquisition and digestion of direct experience? Is the chosen path the gradual or the sudden ascent; the gentle spiral, with seats at chosen intervals from which to admire the view, or the fierce, direct, unpausing 'sudden' way of Zen? Choose as you will, for neither is right or wrong, nor better, and a long way up the hill they are seen to converge at a point which need not trouble us until we reach it. Both paths begin in the worldly life, with what is to hand, and here, and now. Both need the co-ordination of mind and will and all that we have of mental and moral 'guts' to enable us to keep going. Both are a Middle Way between all extremes, in the course of which the inward tension of the mind is slowly raised for the ultimate assault upon illusion, the slaying of the dragon of self, the awakening, when the final veil is torn away, to the light of Enlightenment.

Each way is an approach to the Absolute; in each the effort is perpetual, and is made in the worldly life until right effort has produced the circumstances in which the distraction of that life may be for a time removed while the climber trains for the final assault on Reality. The Theravada is the more solemn way, with something of the Puritan ideal. The Zen way is more joyous, and carefree, and indeed, being frankly irrational, it is free of the concepts, precepts, rules and milestones of the Arhat's introspective concentration. 'Let the mind abide no-where, and alight upon no-thing,' says the Diamond Sutra. And how shall it not when all is indeed an interdiffusion of *sunyata,* Void of all things whatever?

'Move and the Way will open.' This is the heart of Buddhism for it is the first and last word on the Way. The greatest scriptures of the world speak alike of action. The *Bhagavad Gita* is indeed a manual of right action, of the correct tactics in the war within; the *Dhammapada* is a moral philosophy of action, equally applicable without and within. The *Tao Te Ching* is by its very title the Way of Tao, of the virtue of Tao in action. 'When one looks at it, one cannot see it. When one listens to it, one cannot hear it. But when one uses it, it is inexhaustible.' Christ spoke of the mystical unity of the Way. 'I am the Way, the Truth and the Life'; and *The Voice of the Silence*, perhaps the oldest Scripture of them all, makes it clearer still. 'Thou canst not travel on the Path before thou hast become that Path itself.'

Let us arise then, and not only seek experience, direct, immediate experience, but be unafraid when we find it. How? The answer is another question: Who holds you back? Let it be said again, for there is no more to be said. There are two rules upon the Way: Begin, and continue. Asked, 'What is Tao?' a master of Zen replied, 'Walk on'.

The Void is Full

All is a thing which is not something else.
(All that is something else is also a thing).
All things are void.
The Void is the name for an absence of all things.
The Void is also full,
Full of No-thing-ness only.

THE END